TURKEYS

TV
TURKEYS

An Outrageous Look at the Most Preposterous Shows Ever On Television

KEVIN ALLMAN

A Perigee Book

Perigee Books
are published by
The Putnam Publishing Group
200 Madison Avenue
New York, NY 10016

Library of Congress Cataloging-in-Publication Data

Allman, Kevin.
    TV turkeys.

    "A Perigee book."
    1. Television programs—United States.   I. Title.
PN1992.3.U5A46   1987   791.45′75′0973   87-13876
            ISBN 0-399-51404-X

Printed in the United States of America
        1 2 3 4 5 6 7 8 9 10

Acknowledgments

Delving into the television industry is a task best undertaken with as many support systems as possible. Many people have volunteered their time and knowledge to help with this project. They are:

Judy Linden and Eleanor Holdridge at The Putnam Publishing Group, for their long-distance encouragement and whip-cracking.

Arthur and Richard Pine, my unfailingly supportive agents, who graciously donated so much of their time for this book's success.

The staff at the Academy of Motion Picture Arts and Sciences' Margaret Herrick Library, who made the research process infinitely simpler and more pleasurable.

My colleagues at the *Los Angeles Herald-Examiner*, especially Jeannine Stein, David Gritten, Donna Trujillo, Bill Higgins, and Ray Richmond, who put up gracefully with myriad inconveniences.

Bill Farley and Les Magerman, who managed to toil in the entertainment business and still maintain lively senses of humor—and perspective.

Elvis Mitchell, unarguably the best and wittiest television critic in the country. His relentless skewering of the TV business is sorely missed.

Helen Heller, who served as my editor on a similar book at a different publishing house, and remained my friend. Perhaps one day we can work on a project that comes to fruition.

Special thanks are due to the Medved family—Michael, Diane, Harry, Sarah, and Kalby—for a decade of aid in so many areas of my life. They are forgiven for committing the ultimate American heresy: not owning a television set.

And special thanks also to Jim Schmaltz—friend, confidant, and Southern Californian equivalent of Phil Donahue, the only man who can watch *Washington Week in Review* and *The Match Game–Hollywood Squares Hour* with equal relish.

K.A.
Santa Monica, California

For my parents, who will always
prefer C-SPAN to *The Newlywed Game*

Contents

"Art hath an enemy called Ignorance. . . ."
                                    —Ben Jonson

"Television is not the truth. Television is a goddamn
amusement park. Television is a circus, a carnival, a
traveling troupe of acrobats, storytellers, dancers,
singers, jugglers, sideshow freaks, lion tamers and
football players. We're in the boredom-killing business."
                            —Paddy Chayefsky, *Network*

"You're obviously suffering from delusions of *adequacy*!"
                        —Alexis Carrington on *Dynasty*

CHANNEL 1

Tuning In

Why isn't there a Channel 1?

Why isn't there anything good on tonight?

Ah, the eternal questions of television. Fortunately, the first one is easy to answer. In the Dark Ages of TV, long before Geraldo Rivera and Vanna White, there was a Channel 1—in fact, the first NBC station in New York City was on Channel 1. Soon, though, the FCC "revoked" Channel 1, reassigning its broadcast band for use on mobile radios.

Why isn't there anything good on television? In a word, economics. After all, the whole point of the television industry is commercials. Programs are merely the glue that stick product pitches together, and art is totally irrelevant to the process.

David Sarnoff, who formed the National Broadcasting Corporation in 1926, summed up programmers' attitudes in a much-quoted apologia for television. "We're in the same position as a plumber laying a pipe," said Sarnoff. "We're not responsible for what goes through the pipe."

Of course, Sarnoff had no way of knowing how wide this new pipe would be, nor what influence it would have all over the world. And since 1926 TV programmers have—to put it crudely—been laying pipe into every American, night after night after *Thicke of the Night.*

In a programmer's nirvana, a TV audience would be able to watch one ad after another for hours on end, without the unreasonable demand that the commercials be spliced together with some semblance of entertainment. (That's how we were blessed with both MTV and the Home Shopping Network.)

The networks spend millions of dollars each year hiring people to produce not the best, but *the most fiscally promising* programming ideas possible. Sometimes an artistically successful show emerges, but that's really just icing on the quarterly report. In the television industry, art is at best a byproduct of the sales process.

This book celebrates some of the most bizarre programs that the networks have presented over the years, all of them of dubious artistic quality. Some of them ran for twenty years; some are still on the air today. Two of them ran for one telecast apiece before being yanked by an embarrassed network—canceled not due to their wretched quality, but because they were an uncertain or disastrous source of revenue.

Consider: Once upon a time, an executive at CBS gambled that the public would enjoy a slapsticky sitcom about the Nazi stalags, and he was proven right when Americans kept *Hogan's Heroes* on the air for six seasons. It's hard to tell which of the networks' September surprises and midseason droppings the public will accept in any given year, which is why most of the new shows introduced each September are gone within the space of a few months.

Taken together, shows like *Hogan's Heroes, My Mother the Car,* and *Queen for a Day* give a *Mondo Cane*-ish glimpse of the wild world of TV, a world that's sometimes run as cavalierly as a public access station. Could Paddy Chayefsky, dreaming up ideas for *Network,* have conceived of a programmer who would sign a top Japanese recording duo to host a variety show—before discovering that the women couldn't speak English? It happened, and the result was *Pink Lady and Jeff.* Who could have dreamed up a situation comedy about a man who discovers his mother reincarnated as a rickety old automobile?

Perhaps the question isn't *why,* but *why not?* The bad-taste bathos of *Queen for a Day* held homemakers in its sway for years, making millions of dollars in the process. *The Newlywed Game* and *The New Newlywed Game* have been drawing viewers off and on for two decades. Even a concept as ridiculous as *The Flying Nun* was a carefully calculated risk, based on strong marketing knowledge indicating that the public wanted to see Sally Field clad in a nun's habit as she dangled from piano wires. And some transcendent TV trash has even managed to enter the pop culture history books. *The Gong Show* was a national craze for a few years, and spawned the verb "gonged" as an expression of contempt.

We watch this stuff, and we love it. Art and longevity aren't the point. Hamlet has been soliloquizing for centuries, but he's never topped the best-seller lists. When it comes to profitable entertainment, the public has always preferred to curl up with

Valley of the Dolls and a bag of potato chips, while *Hee Haw* and *Let's Make a Deal* play softly in the background.

Why fight it? Why not celebrate it instead? Couch potatoes all over the world would sooner cut off their right arms than skip a single installment of their favorite soaps, or miss the chance to see that *Flying Nun* episode for the eighteenth time.

Channel 1 is signing off. As the snow descends and the diagonal lines obscure the screen, we can flip to Channel 2 and begin our search for signs of intelligent life in the television universe.

CHANNEL 2

False Starts:
The Humble Beginnings of Your Favorite Stars

TV exposure is a great way for any actor to kick off his or her career; many stars like Clint Eastwood, Burt Reynolds, Lily Tomlin, and Goldie Hawn got their big breaks in such unpromising programs as *Rawhide*, *Dan August*, and *Rowan & Martin's Laugh-In*.

Still, for others, early TV exposure was a handicap that had to be overcome through years of hard work. The thought of Sally "Gidget" Field becoming a two-time Oscar winner would have seemed as ridiculous to early TV viewers as . . . as the thought of, say, *Death Valley Days'* Ronald Reagan becoming President of the United States.

Tuning in to Channel 2 on our voyage down the tube, we find that true talent can rise, phoenixlike, even from the ashes of television's worst burnt offerings.

The Flying Nun
ABC: 1967–1970

Sally Field has spent her career creating many memorable roles, including the title characters in *Norma Rae* and *Sybil*, and the object of James Garner's affections in *Murphy's Romance*. Still, one image of Field lingers in the collective American memory—the picture of a squeaky-clean, cuter-than-cute girl in a nun's habit, sailing through the air with barely concealed wires guiding her flight. For three years on network television and nearly two decades in syndication, Field has been cruising the friendly skies as *The Flying Nun*.

Field was discovered by ABC, which was laying plans for a weekly series based on the popular *Gidget* films and concurrently began a search for a thoroughly modern surfer chick to play the title role of the boy-crazy girl-midget. Unlike the James Bond flicks, each *Gidget* film featured a different girl in the title role. Columbia Pictures, which produced the series, thought Field could fill Sandra Dee's sandals admirably,

and soon Field—with no formal acting experience—was the star of the most highly touted sitcom of the 1965 season. And while critics thought the show a wipeout, most of them thought Field herself to be a real discovery, describing her with the adjective that would soon be her signature—*cute*.

Gidget lasted only a year, but its loyal fans wrote more than 100,000 letters to the network, begging the ABC powers that were to let Gidge keep surfing the waves endlessly. Similar letter-writing campaigns might have saved *Star Trek* and *Cagney and Lacey*, but the ploy couldn't spare *Gidget* from drowning in the ratings.

Still, the consensus between the television industry and the public was that Sally Field was the cutest thing to hit the home screen since Annette's Mousekabust busted out of *The Mickey Mouse Club*.

"I hate being cute," Field complained to a magazine reporter. "When someone says I'm cute, I want

She's adorable when she gets mad. Sally Field was the cutest thing in Convent San Tanco as *The Flying Nun*. Marge Redmond (right), who went on to push Cool Whip in innumerable commercials, looks on.

to throw right up.'' And some sour-puss critics claimed that she had the same effect on them.

Cute, scrubbed, asexual: These were Field's strengths, and it was only natural that soon after *Gidget* left the air in 1966 that ABC found a new project for her. The network and Screen Gems Productions (the firm that had also come up with *Gidget*) had purchased the rights to make a television series out of *The Fifteenth Pelican*, a novel by a Baltimore woman Tere Rios. The book was

about a nun. A nun who could fly.

Most industry types might have sneered at the possibility of making a series with such a ludicrous premise, but veteran producer Harry Ackerman saw some potential in it. ABC's biggest sitcom hit at the time was *Bewitched*, the story of a suburban housewife with magical powers, and Ackerman had guided the show to success. Others had done well with silly supernatural plots, including *My Favorite Martian* (Ray Walston as a magical extraterrestrial) and *I*

Dream of Jeannie, with Barbara Eden as a genie with magic powers (but no navel).

Cannily, Ackerman noticed that nun themes had always done well at the box office. *The Sound of Music* and *The Trouble With Angels* were current hits, and past successes had included *The Nun's Story* with Audrey Hepburn, *Lilies of the Field, The Bells of St. Mary's,* and even *The Singing Nun,* which featured a twinkly Debbie Reynolds whaling away at a guitar while she crooned "Dominique."

Most surprisingly, there hadn't been a TV series to capitalize on this moneymaking trend by using a nun in the lead role. Screen Gems was resistant to the notion of an overly religious program, but ABC president Tom Moore saw the logic of America's nunmania, and, more importantly, saw Field as the perfect choice to get into the habit.

Field turned the offer down flat, having decided that the field of sitcoms was no place for her. Though ABC went through with the show and another actress, they continued negotiating with Sally Field. She finally came around while the first episode was already being made, resulting in another actress being excommunicated from the role. ABC crossed its corporate fingers and hoped that public and sponsor response would justify all the fuss.

In addition to Field, the cast for the pilot featured veteran character actors, including Marge Redmond (who would go on to greater fame as the proprietress of Sarah Tucker's Inn in innumerable Cool Whip commercials) as Sister Jacqueline, Field's best friend. Madeleine Sherwood was her foil, the authoritarian Mother Superior, who wasn't enthralled to discover that one of her charges could fly. (The aeronautics occurred only when the Puerto Rican trade winds buoyed her stiff cornette, the Spruce-Gooselike hat worn by the nuns in the series.)

Also in the cast was Alejandro Rey, who played a rich rogue who owned a nearby casino/disco; he and Field often engaged in some tender byplay on the show. The producers, on advisement from real nuns, never let Field and Rey actually flirt; after all, if Barbara Eden still couldn't display her navel on NBC, ABC wasn't about to admit that a nun might have sexual attractions.

When the two-part pilot was aired for test audiences, the approval ratings went through the roof. ABC quickly made the newly christened *Flying Nun* one of the centerpieces of its fall 1967 lineup, positioning it safely between two established hits, *Batman* and *Bewitched*. Not coincidentally, the stars of the other two series often did some flying on their respective shows—although Batman needed a Batrope and Elizabeth Montgomery some artfully concealed piano wire.

ABC announced its fall schedule,

Not even the suave playboy Carlos (Alejandro Rey) could penetrate Sally Field's convent walls; God was her only copilot.

proudly presenting its new series to the public—*and everyone laughed! The Singing Nun* was one thing, but a flying nun? Johnny Carson single-handedly got the nation talking about *The Flying Nun* by mentioning the yet-to-be-seen show in his monologue one night. Carson joked that a competing network intended to counterprogram with a new series called *Space Rabbi*.

Actually, no one at ABC admitted to liking the title *The Flying Nun*, and cast members claimed that they tried to think up an alternate but came up empty. ("It's so eeuucchh!" said Sally Field, demonstrating once again why she was the cutest thing on TV.)

Eeuucchh, it was assumed, would have been the official Catholic position on the show, but the Pope never really got around to issuing a papal bull on the subject of Sally Field. Some nuns from the Southern California archdiocese were called upon to view the first episodes and offer suggestions, and their views on what the show was all about were predictably diverse: many saw *The Flying Nun* as an attempt to "humanize" their orders, while others saw it as a trivialization of Catholicism. Others just saw it as *eeuucchh*. One nun, Sister Mary Benigna, did, however, feel that "Sally Field is more believable as a nun than Debbie Reynolds." This opinion had nothing to do with the fact that Field was never involved in a love triangle with Eddie Fisher and Elizabeth Taylor; Sister Mary Benigna simply felt that "Sally is so clean and well-scrubbed looking." Diplomatically, Sister Mary Benigna avoided mentioning the by-now anathema "C" word.

On the old *Superman* show, the producers had solved the flying problem by using the exact same shot on every episode, saving time and money. On *The Flying Nun*, the flying effects were a bit more sophisticated, even if the scripts weren't. Strung up on a harness attached to piano wires, the diminutive star was hung from a crane attached to the back of a truck, and the whole rickety conveyance drove off, leaving a cameraman to photograph Sally and the scenery and the wind in her hair. On more dangerous shots, a stunt double was used, but most of the time viewers were treated to a shot of Sally Field, white habit billowing in the air, "flying" through the Puerto Rican coun-tryside. Only when the sunlight glanced off the wires was the illusion spoiled—once every show or so.

A summerlong promotion campaign emphasizing the flying rather than the nuns appeared to pay off. By the time the show debuted on September 7, 1967, it captured a large portion of the Thursday viewing audience. In a few short months, it was regularly scoring in the Top 20, and had been parlayed into ABC's only new hit of the 1967–68 season.

The good ratings were in no way due to the sophomoric scripts, most of which should have inspired their authors to revoke their Writers Guild memberships and say an Act of Contrition. One episode found Sister Bertrille writing tunes for a rock group that came to Puerto Rico for some tuneful inspiration, only to find her happy song turned into a sixties version of heavy metal—much to the sisters' chagrin. The chirpy nun also wasn't above playing poker with church attendance as the stakes, or becoming the inamorata of a real pelican in heat. (The randy bird must have heard those stories about why Catholic girls wear reflective shoes.)

The network continually promised that the scripts would improve, and actress Madeleine Sherwood finally got so fed up with the situation that she enrolled in a home-correspondence writing course. Ever-helpful Sister Mary Benigna—who had applauded Field's scrubbed face—suggested to the producers that they should hold a scriptwriting contest among real nuns to add some authenticity to the show, but producers Ackerman and William Sackheim hailed Mary's idea and promptly passed on the suggestion.

Why was *The Flying Nun*, with its preposterous premise and substandard scripts, such a hit? Madeleine Sherwood had a unique opinion: "People follow Catholics like they follow a ball game," she analogized. "Who's for celibacy? And who's against the Pill?"

Sherwood's vision of the historic Vatican II conference as just another variation on a Redskins–49ers matchup wasn't shared by everyone. Costar Marge Redmond felt differently, citing curiosity as a factor for the high ratings: "Nobody really has known what does go on in a convent." (Catfights with rosaries? Lesbian acts during Vespers?) While this might be the reason that people continue to seek out women's prison films, it hardly explained *The Flying Nun* phenomenon—after all, the

Chelsea Brown, the *Laugh-In* go-go dancer, guest starred on one episode as the convent's new secretary.

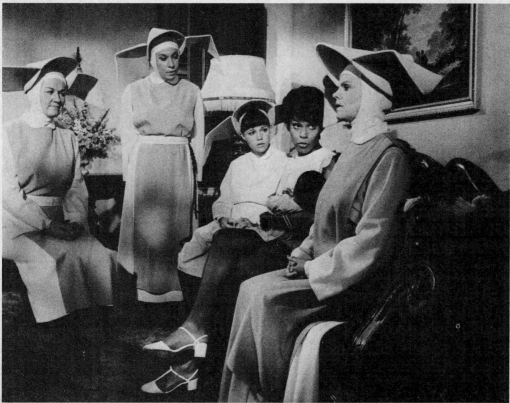

A chaste handshake was the most that Sally Field and Alejandro Rey could share on *The Flying Nun*.

show wasn't entitled *Nuns Behind Bars*.

Still, there were some final adjustments to be made, especially in the character of the Mother Superior; Catholics didn't want her to be portrayed as Nancy Sinatra in a habit, but still they thought the character to be (in the words of producer Bill Sackheim) "too flinty and hard."

"We have tried to give her warmth, to soften the character, and make her more human," Sackheim reassured the media. "The reaction to Sally is extraordinarily positive. They [Catholics] have responded very favorably to the fact she's a human being," Sackheim added, as if a nun was little more than a Stepford-Wife-of-God.

"The people say, 'Enough of this syrupy molasses,'" Sackheim concluded.

Field, ever vigilant against her own genetic cuteness, agreed. "The reaction from Catholics to the series is fantastic. They are glad at long last to see a nun portrayed as a human being, getting away from being a symbol, and kind of hip. I don't want to be sweet, saccharine, and syrupy. Any line that's too sweet, I don't say it.

"I don't play her like a nun," Field added, somewhat enigmatically. "There is never a thought I'm in a convent."

True enough; a look at Sister Bertrille's impetuosity and talent for getting into sitcom scrapes reveals that *The Flying Nun* could have been known as *Hail Gidget*. Although the bathing suits were replaced by habits, and surfboards by Bibles, the show was basically Gidget Goes to the Vatican.

It hit immediately. A November 1967 survey revealed that *The Flying Nun* was the Number One show on television—for children aged six to eleven. In the 18–34 and 50+ groups; *Nun* didn't rank at all; apparently the oldsters found the idea pretty rank in itself.

Younger viewers, however, made the show—and made *The Flying Nun* the only new series that year to crack the Top 20 in the ratings. Tapping into that audience, Field, Redmond, and Sherwood hit the recording studio to wax a version of "He's Got the Whole World in His Hands." An airline even contacted Field regarding a series of commercial spots with the slogan "Fly the Planes that Nuns Who Fly for a Living Fly!"

In September 1968, Field got married, and the costume department was quickly scrambling for ways to hide two consecutive pregnancies inside Sister Bertrille's habit.

One interesting byproduct of all this exposure to old-time religion was Sally Field's announcement that she had been led back to God through her role in the show. The Lord works in mysterious ways, but the puckish editors of *Esquire* magazine saw fit to include her Hollywood conversion in their 1968 roundup of the annual Dubious Achievement Awards.

God as *The Flying Nun*'s copilot notwithstanding, the gimmick had to wear off eventually. The ratings plummeted back down to earth with such ferocity that the show was canceled after three years. This was no disappointment to Field, who forswore television series for two TV movies designed to expand her range. It wasn't that easy to break her image of airborne NutraSweet. After another terrible sitcom, *The Girl with Something Extra* (about a young newlywed saddled with the twin problems of ESP and a marriage to John Davidson), it wasn't until the TV film *Sybil* and the feature film *Norma Rae* that the star got some respect.

In later interviews, the former Sister Bertrille became more outspoken about her *Nun* days. "I was fed up being a joke. I was stuck, a totally undiscovered talent with a well-known name. Everybody figured I was drowning in effervescence; an hour with me was enough to justify an insulin injection."

By the time that she accepted her second Academy Award with the deathless words, "You like me! You really *like* me!", the days of Sally-bashing were over, and the "C" word forgotten. Twenty years later, the stigma—not to mention the stigmata—was finally gone.

Cos

ABC: 1976

It's hard to remember a time when megasuccessful Bill Cosby wasn't Dr. Cliff Huxtable on the home screen. There was a period of two months in 1976, though, when it seemed that the magic had worn off his particular brand of family-style humor. That was *Cos*, a variety show that seemed like a series version of one of his Jell-O Pudding commercials stretched out to feature length with the addition of pious guest stars, subtle moral lessons, and, of course, saccharine moppets.

Cos was designed as ABC's entry in the early Sunday slot of 7 P.M., which was pretty much ruled by *60 Minutes* and *The Wonderful World of Disney*. And Cosby took this Family Hour duty seriously—but not quite as seriously as he took himself. Speaking on the upcoming show, he said: "The Family Hour has to do with something very, very technical. It has to do with using the tube to address itself to educational values, to teaching, to subjects that have to do with morals."

This vaguely pompous pronouncement might have had something to do with the fact that the comedian had recently received a doctorate in education from the University of Massachusetts, and a few media pundits were beginning to allude that the sheepskin was swelling the good doctor's head. (Indeed, Cosby refers to himself once in the credits of *The Cosby Show* as "Dr. William H. Cosby, Jr., Ed.D.")

Kay Gardella of the New York *Daily News*, a Cosby supporter in the past, cautioned, "Of late Cosby . . . gives the impression that he's carrying the responsibility for all the young people of the world on his shoulders. . . . It tends to inject a little of the preacher into the comedian. Dangerous inflation of opinion can result, and must be guarded against."

What responsibility? Curing famine with the distribution of Jell-O to the Third World? The biggest slap at the comic came from *The Village Voice*, however, which cruelly (and

Cos and Effect: America's favorite TV dad, Bill Cosby, fell flat on his Huxtable in the 1976 variety show *Cos*.

accurately) limned Cos's devolution from humorist to moralist:

"Cosby has become unfunny in recent years, a monotonous young fogey capitalizing wherever he can on his splendiferous teacher thing. . . . He has evolved into a kind of self-parodying sap."

These were the cards that were stacked against the premiere of *Cos,* and, unfortunately, Cosby did nothing to dispel the predictions of these dire Cassandras. The premise of the variety show turned out to be a re-hash of Art Linkletter's *House Party,* where Kids Said the Darnedest Things With a Little Coaching from Cos. The guest stars (Cindy Williams, Bruce Jenner, the rock group Chicago) seemed unearthed from some mid-seventies time capsule, squarely between earth shoes and Bicentennial macramé fashions. And Bill Cosby's monologues, which were so fresh and down-to-earth in the sixties, were now thinly disguised bits of social significance and condescending advice.

Variety's review was about as kind as they came, calling *Cos* "an uneven mixture of clever and silly material . . . deliberately tailored for tots' brief attention spans." The *L.A. Times* buffaloed Bill, giving it to him with both barrels and saying that *Cos* had "the look of a show in the death throes of a ten-year run. . . . The lackluster style of the comedy-variety hour was set by Bill Cosby, who moved from bit to bit without energy or enthusiasm. . . . The sketches were uniformly vapid and the performers carried on as if the joke were on the audience—for watching." The newspaper then summed up the show as "warmed-over TV variety-show pulp."

But it was Cleveland Amory, resident curmudgeon of *TV Guide,* whose ill temper was never shown off to such blistering advantage: "Cosby came on the way he does in those commercials in which he persuades little children to eat their canned peas. Sixty seconds of Cosby being cutesy-poo in a commercial is one thing; sixty minutes of the same every Sunday night is another. With Cosby's new Ph.D. in education . . . perhaps he feels a professional obligation to be boring." (Don't critics say the darnedest things?)

The star of the show seemed sour on the whole prospect himself—especially when the Black Writers' Caucus made a hue and cry over the fact that only two of the show's twelve writers were black. "I'm really on my countdown to retirement," he groused. "My first series, *I Spy,* ran three years. *The Bill Cosby Show* lasted two years. My first variety hour lasted one year. And this show? If I'm lucky, it will last thirteen weeks."

Thirteen weeks? Guess again. *Cos* was ranking sixty-second out of 62 shows for the week, and ratings for *60 Minutes* had never been higher. "I've got a thirteen-segment commitment," Cosby said, "but the way it's going, the next time around they'll sign me to a one-hour special and take a look at the ratings after thirty minutes to decide if they want to pick up the second half."

Although the network was in for thirteen weeks, *Cos* actually only lasted seven, and probably would have been forgotten in less time than that if it weren't for one altercation between Bill Cosby and Tommy Smothers.

As *Cos* limped its way toward oblivion, Cosby attended a party at the Playboy Mansion West. Smothers allegedly approached the mercurial comic to congratulate him on *Cos*. Exactly what happened next has been disputed, but everyone saw the result: Tommy Smothers ended up flat on the floor.

Cuddly Cliff Huxtable in the Sodom and Gomorrah atmosphere of Hugh Hefner's Playpen? Cos the Jell-O junkie engaging in fisticuffs? Are these the "educational values" and "subjects that have to do with morals" that Cosby spoke of?

Of course, none of it mattered a fig eight years later, when Cosby's return to TV was the biggest small-screen arrival since Little Ricky on *I Love Lucy*. But the next time that America's favorite superhuman humorist forgoes the comedy and starts to scat with some old-fashioned sermonizing, bored viewers might want to drift into a reverie: the sight of one Smothers Brother, laid out like a Pudding Pop on the floor of the Playboy Mansion.

Thicke of the Night

**SYNDICATED OVER THE METROMEDIA NETWORK:
1983–1984**

How bad can a show be?

So bad that its own star actually *faints* while watching one of the first episodes.

The star who preferred to pass out than to pass the buck was Alan Thicke, Canada's answer to Johnny Carson and Paul Hogan. And the show that brought on such a violent reaction was *Thicke of the Night*, an abortive late-night comedy-variety show designed to knock the silk hat and the high ratings off of Johnny Carson.

"It was comedy aerobics," remembered Thicke. "Culminating in one huge groin pull."

Thicke's kick in the, er, *sensibilities*, began on January 10, 1983, when programming czar Fred Silverman called a major press conference in Bel Air, California. Silverman had led both CBS and ABC to the top of the ratings, earning him the nickname "The Man with the Golden Gut." Unfortunately, the gut had turned to pyrite when he tried to do the same thing at NBC, resulting in

megaflops like *Pink Lady and Jeff* and *Supertrain*. By 1983, he had been fired by NBC and had formed his own production company. The cornerstone of this effort was to be *Thicke of the Night*, a wild and woolly cross between the *Tonight* show and *Saturday Night Live*. And the man who was going to butt heads with Carson was Alan Thicke.

Alan who? the public wanted to know.

Thicke had worked behind the scenes on many successful American programs, including *The Flip Wilson Show* and *Fernwood 2-Night*, before taking on his own daytime program in Canada. Ratings zoomed when Canadian women and girls found Thicke's combination of dark hair, dazzling smile, and passable singing voice too much to resist.

That was all Thicke was expected to bring to the States. It was Silverman who had the tough job: to make Alan Thicke a household name in America by the time the show debuted in September. "There's great

Alan Thicke chomps down on what must have been a piece of humble pie during the run of *Thicke of the Night*.

interest in Alan because most people don't know him here,'' Silverman boasted hopefully. ''It's kind of a David and Goliath story.''

Up in Canada, where Thicke was all too well known to TV critics, the consensus was that the host was a perfectly affable guy, but a little bit too white-bread for their tastes.

''He's basically bland,'' said Rita Zekas of the Toronto *Star*. ''He's like a John Davidson, Ken-doll clone.''

As it turned out, Thicke's saving

grace (and the quality that saved him after the show failed) was a wise, self-deprecating sense of humor that took into account his shortcomings.

But still, the question remained: What did Alan Thicke *do*?

"The key to the potential of my success is that I do so many things—and none of them threateningly well, that I'm a master of 'B' talents, that I'm not discernibly talented in any singular area, but I'm better than your Uncle Herb at a party," explained Thicke.

It was established early on, then, that no one—not even Thicke himself—was quite sure just *what* he did. This was quite acceptable for talk-show guests—witness the continued success of the Gabor sisters—but it was certainly a deviation from the norm to have a host who did a little of everything and a lot of nothing.

As *Thicke of the Night* rumbled on toward its debut, a cast of repertory comedians was assembled, including popular stand-up comedian Richard Belzer, former *Saturday Night Live* regular Gilbert Gottfried, and Chloe Webb (the future star of *Sid and Nancy*).

Since neither the producers nor the show's host had any sense of what *Thicke of the Night* was supposed to be about, however, the program amounted to nothing more than a comedy garage sale—and the set looked like one as well. It was a cross between the rough-edged *Saturday Night Live* studio, the homey couch-and-desk setup of every other talk show on the air, and a cluttered construction site—rather appropriate, since *Thicke of the Night* was constantly under construction for the length of its run.

Meanwhile, Fred Silverman had done his work, trumpeting to the media that the coming of *Thicke of the Night* was an event equal to the Beatles appearing on *The Ed Sullivan Show*. All over the country, billboards announced the arrival of Alan Thicke. Radio spots reminded everyone that a new epoch in television was dawning. Newspapers cleaned up on *Thicke of the Night* advertising. Most of all, the TV stations that would carry *Thicke* soaked the airwaves with an old-fashioned saturation campaign, building high expectations about the new show and its new host-with-the-most.

While no one was really betting that *Thicke of the Night* would put a wooden stake into the heart of *Tonight,* most industry pundits predicted that it couldn't help but draw fairly respectable ratings. Until the first Monday in September 1983, though, it was hard to see that the Young Turk was really a Young Turkey.

Fred Silverman was certainly in programmer's heaven the week before *Thicke* debuted. He had managed to get the show into 80 percent of American markets, with more than 100 stations signed to carry the show.

More than 30 of those were network affiliates, and a dozen of them were NBC-owned. If Thicke was to fail, it wouldn't be for lack of exposure.

Sure enough, lack of exposure had nothing to do with it.

In L.A., which is often a bellwether for what will be considered hip in the rest of the country, *Thicke of the Night* drew a thin rating of 2.7, with only 10 percent of the viewing audience tuned in.

And it wasn't exactly up against stiff competition. Alan Thicke and Company wilted against a less-than-powerhouse Carson rerun on NBC, *Nightline* on ABC, and CBS's offering of highlights from the U.S. Open golf tournament. (When you can't beat televised *golf*, you're in big trouble.)

Even sadder, Alan and his Thickers had assembled what they thought was a dynamite, everything-but-the-kitchen-sink lineup for the inaugural broadcast. From the critical response and the public indifference, a ninety-minute film clip of the kitchen sink might have inspired more fever.

There were interviews with three semi-heavyweights, including Joan Collins, onetime John Lennon mistress May Pang, and the ever-popular Barry Manilow. More than a few people wondered if having the likes of Manilow was Thicke's idea of hip. What was next? Baking brownies with the Osmonds? After all, a soap queen, a low-budget Britt Ekland, and a soporific rocker

weren't about to catapult Thicke into the stratosphere with the younger generation.

A few purported comedy skits reached depths that hadn't even been plumbed on the most incoherent, drug-soaked *Saturday Night Live* episodes. Most embarrassing of all, Silverman himself opened the show, introducing himself as a—yuk yuk yuk—*guest host* for Alan Thicke. The effect was more pathetic than irreverent; it was like Judd Nelson taking a public poke at Laurence Oliver.

When the show ground to a halt well after midnight, the most memorable moment had turned out to be during Thicke's opening, where he modestly announced that he wasn't nearly as talented "as Silverman has been saying in the papers." Amen to that.

Just another flop, it seemed, but *Thicke of the Night* soon developed a personality as dangerous and indestructible as Jason in the *Friday the 13th* movies: The Show That Refused to Die.

Ratings dropped like a concrete soufflé for the first month, and it became increasingly clear that *Thicke of the Night* was really Thicke in the Head. Still, there had been flops on television before; that was no novelty. But as the first few episodes continued to cross the airwaves, looking for a television set that would pick them up, Thicke began to be a national joke.

A. C. Nielsen and company provided the first major embarrassment that set the TV community talking: Less than a month later, *Thicke of the Night* registered a *zero* share in Philadelphia. There were so few sets in the city tuned in to the program during its broadcast that the rating service couldn't find it registered on its meters.

Fred Silverman, meanwhile, put on a happy face for the public. When the show soared to a mighty rating of 2 in November, Silverman told the press, "It's very encouraging . . . we see things building."

Whatever those things were, they certainly weren't the ratings. Later that month, it became obvious

Though Alan Thicke was smiling in his office during the debut week of *Thicke*, he later claimed that he had literally fainted in horror while watching his own show—the night before this picture was taken.

that the Philadelphia syndrome was spreading like Nielsen cancer. By mid-November, *Thicke* did the exact same thing in Los Angeles. Although the first fifteen minutes of the broadcast drew a puny 8/10 of a rating point in Hollywood, the remainder of the show fell off the Nielsen meters, officially registering as the Big Zero in the Big Orange. (The ever helpful Nielsen statisticians ground salt into the wound by estimating that perhaps the figure had gone down to 1/10 by the end of the show.)

Alan Thicke, perhaps still nursing the bruises from the night he passed out, was more than willing to eat crow pie in the public eye. When asked what he thought of the summerlong publicity that touted him as a successor to Carson, he replied, "I don't have regrets as much as I have suicidal tendencies over it."

No one expected that Silverman would keep things going with ratings that had to be tabulated under an electron microscope, but against all odds, *Thicke of the Night* was renewed on January 17, 1984, for another thirteen weeks. Another 65 shows. Another 97½ hours of Thicke-headedness.

A few stations politely declined to continue carrying the program (including Philadelphia), but approximately sixty broadcasters signed on for another quarter-year. Meanwhile, the show's star was telling the press that he found the show "an undoable, unproduceable, overproduced ap-proach that made consistency impossible."

Silverman came up with the idea of throwing in the towel for the first hundred or so shows, and revamping the show's advertising campaign to emphasize a new, improved, lean, mean *Thicke of the Night* machine.

New, improved, lemon-freshened, low-tar, or pina-colada scented, it still stank. The major changes were the departure of many of the faceless cast members, and the addition of Thicke's wife Gloria Loring as a frequent guest, who would warble songs in a manner as innocuous and bland as her husband's. In sheer desperation, *Hot Seat* host Wally George became a once-a-week regular, spouting his God and America opinions to the boos of the audience, turning the new improved *Thicke of the Night* into The Alan Horror Picture Show.

Nine months later, the brain-dead patient was finally laid to rest (after some more zero ratings), and production executive Lawrence Gershman laid the blame squarely where it belonged—on the heads of *the station affiliates.*

"We're regretfully not going forward with any additional episodes," Gershman told the press. "The support at the station level is not there." (Fred Silverman, apparently the sort of man who prefers weddings to funerals, was not present at the announcement. "We've informed him and he's cognizant," said Gershman.)

As a suburban father on *Growing Pains,* Alan Thicke (seen here with Joanna Kerns) gained the critical respect denied him throughout the run of *Thicke of the Night.*

The hapless Alan Thicke, meanwhile, was hit with a double whammy. The same day that his show was canceled, he picked up the morning paper only to discover that his wife had filed for divorce.

Without telling him.

"When you say it's one of the worst shows in TV history," groaned Thicke later, "that's going to be on my tombstone. . . . I don't even drink, and if there was ever a year I could have . . . We'd have six minutes with Martin Sheen, and then we'd spend twelve minutes on a belly dancer with a one-dollar bill in her navel."

Still, fortunes in the TV industry turn around quickly. Within two years, the man whose name was a national joke was finished licking his wounds and had been tapped to play a wholesome TV father in a wholesome TV family comedy called *Growing Pains*. It became one of the surprise hits of the 1985 season, and restored some of Alan Thicke's credibility in the television capital.

And the final nail in the coffin of *Thicke of the Night* came in November 1986, when Thicke had a guest role in an NBC reunion special of *Perry Mason*. In the show, he played an obnoxious talk-show host, and actually got murdered on the air.

Thicke's reaction?

"It seems redundant."

Premises, Premises:
High-Concept Shows for Lowbrow Audiences

There's a true story about an aspiring television writer called into the offices of a major network to discuss his idea for a new situation comedy.

"You'll love it," the journeyman writer enthused. "It's all about a horse that can talk, but only his owner can hear him, and they get into all sorts of adventures. . . ."

The television executive, a kindly man, chose his words carefully. "But there was already a show like that," he said. "It was called *Mr. Ed.*"

"No, this is completely different," explained the writer. "The horse only speaks Italian."

If this show had made it to the air, it would no doubt be found here on Channel 3, home to the strangest and most banal premises ever to disgrace the picture tube.

We Got It Made

NBC: 1983–1984

If *Three* was *Company*, what was five? Dumb, titillating, sophomoric, double entendre humor, that's what. The hit ABC sitcom featured one horny guy, one dumb blonde, and one suspicious brunette. *We Got It Made* was a pallid copy of *Three's Company* that went it two better: one dumb blonde, two suspicious brunettes, and two libidinous dudes driven by equal doses of testosterone and locker room humor.

Who could have created such an Abominable Snowjob? Since it wasn't a game show, it wasn't Chuck Barris. It could only be Fred Silverman, who departed NBC with the chance to develop this sappy sitcom for the network.

The premise was as ridiculous as it was simple. Two Manhattan bachelors, one a hunk (Matt McCoy) and the other a wackyzanynutty goofball (Tom Villard), hire a maid to clean their apartment. Whoopsie! The most qualified applicant looks nothing like Shirley Booth or Ann B. Davis; she's a vacuum-wielding 38D cup who would be lucky to have an IQ to match. Mickey the maid also has a cotton candy bouffant like Loni Anderson's and anatomy that would make any man scatter his clothes on the floor just for the joy of watching her bend over to pick them up.

All this is just swell with the guys, the sort of men who probably collect back issues of *Gallery* and *Swank*. It's not so hunky-dory with their plainer girlfriends (Stephanie Kramer and Bonnie Urseth), who expect Mickey to be a mouse instead of a bombshell.

And the high jinks (or low jinks, as the case may be) begin. To the uninitiated, the process of creating a show like *We Got It Made* might seem as easy as ingesting equal parts of Ex-Lax and LSD, but *We Got It Made* was a high-concept/lowbrow affair based on an investment of thousands of hours—and hundreds of thousands of dollars.

As with *Three's Company*, the young, attractive cast were to be unknowns who would, with a little luck,

Mickey the maid was no mouse in NBC's failed ripoff of *Three's Company, We Got It Made. NBC*

Maid to Order: Perky Teri Copley, star of *We Got it Made,* told the press: "I really don't care to be extremely intelligent." That was fortunate, because the jokes on the show stemmed largely from Teri's T & A (and that doesn't stand for Talent and Abilities).

be built into major stars within a year. (One of the girlfriends, Stephanie Kramer, actually went on to play Fred Dryer's Dirty Harriet–sidekick on *Hunter*.) The pivotal role of Mickey was the most difficult to cast until producers stumbled upon a fresh-faced aspiring actress named Teri Copley, who was working at the Two Guys From Italy pizzeria in suburban Westchester, California.

What Copley lacked in dramatic experience she made up for in chest measurements, and a subsequent screen test shown to the public indicated that Copley's sizeable talents were vastly appealing to sitcom audiences. And Copley, unlike other sex symbols such as Jayne Mansfield (who insisted that her IQ was somewhere in the 170 range), harbored no illusions about her intellect.

"I'm not a rocket scientist, but I'm not a stupid person," she told the press, adding, "I really don't care to be extremely intelligent."

That was fortunate for Teri, because the peepee-caca humor and the spun-polyester conflicts of *We Got It Made* made *Three's Company* look like a naturalistic comedy. Journalists Mark Christensen and Cameron Stauth, on hand for the taping of the pilot, noted: "The biggest laugh of the night was when a toilet seat, under the impact of pressing thighs, played the first four notes of 'Here Comes the Bride.' The second-biggest laugh was when it did it again."

NBC, seeing *We Got It Made* as its best bet for the new TV season, even moved the premiere up a couple of weeks in order to get the show off right. *We Got It Made* was also heavily promoted in on-air teases which featured Copley, in black stockings and red stilettos, breathing: "Hi! I just got hired as a live-in maid by two guys. Do I service them both? Maybe even at the same time?? To find out—be there!"

Unfortunately for Copley and company, the American public showed a surprising demonstration of good taste and wasn't there. Although market research had indicated that *We Got It Made* stood a great chance of becoming a hit, it fared only middling well in the ratings and had to be moved from its original time slot. (Originally it preceded *Cheers*, which did neither comedy a favor.) *We Got It Made*, thanks to an uncharacteristic display of common sense among TV viewers, was yanked within six months of its premiere, leaving the horny bachelors on the show unsatisfied forever. Apparently, when it came to maids, the viewing audience preferred bawling Beulah and hapless Hazel to Mickey's mammaries.

Just Our Luck

ABC: 1983

Rip-offs seldom work in TV, but programmers never learn. Witness the creation (and quick self-destruction) of *Just Our Luck,* an *I Dream of Jeannie* steal with *Amos 'n Andy* undertones. Instead of the voluptuous Barbara Eden in a harem costume, the genie in *Just Our Luck* was a jivey black guy who could only come from the imagination of TV's white scriptwriters.

Black actors have traditionally gotten the short end of the Hollywood stick. With a few notable exceptions (Bill Cosby, Diahann Carroll), most black TV actors have only progressed from playing servants to playing "uppity" or "streetwise" types on shows like *Starsky and Hutch, Get Christie Love!,* and *The Jeffersons.* Call it what you want—justifiably aggrieved black actors, woefully unrepresented in the industry as a whole, think that it's the same old shuck and jive.

Activists and aesthetes could both agree on *Just Our Luck,* however, which was as stupidly plotted as it was subtly offensive. The writers transplanted the *I Dream of Jeannie* plot from the Florida coast to the California coast, and cast Richard Gilliland as a Wonder Bread TV weatherman named Keith who likes to jog along Venice Beach. Possessing the physical dexterity of that other great TV weatherman, Willard Scott, Keith naturally Reeboks his way right into a souvenir stand. The proprietor, a proponent of the "You break it, you buy it" philosophy, demands that he purchase a mysterious old bottle that falls to the boardwalk.

After getting it home, our adorable weatherman leaves the bottle within knocking-over distance of his cat, an animal as klutzy as he is. One flick of a paw, the bottle topples over, and out pops Shabu, faithful genie to the sort of historical personages that regularly drop in on Steve Allen's *Meeting of Minds* (see Channel 9: Shooting Stars)—Napoleon Bonaparte, Cleopatra, and our hero.

Naturally, Shabu gets Keith

into the same tired Wacky Scrapes and Zany Antics familiar to TV viewers; after all, isn't that what a genie is supposed to do for his (er, uh, the scriptwriters don't like this word, but), ummm—*master*?

"Shabu doesn't have a master because he doesn't believe in masters," explained T.K. Carter, who had gone from costarring with Dan Aykroyd in *Dr. Detroit* to the role of the subservient sorcerer.

"This isn't going to be anything like *I Dream of Jeannie*," he added, which came as news to both the critics and the viewers of the show—all of whom castigated *Just Our Luck* as ABC's most blatant rip-off since *Battlestar Galactica*.

Bigger problems were brewing as well when the NAACP joined the fray: *Just Our Luck*, for all its ethnically balanced protestations, turned out to have a lily-white team of ten writers turning out the dialogue. Carter was subsequently caught in the middle of an NAACP-threatened advertisers' boycott and his loyalties to the show, and he expressed his opinion that the genie was no weenie.

"I made it clear that I won't do that jive routine," he said, "acting like some cat in a black El Dorado, drinking a Kool-Aid daiquiri with a hat as big as a house. . . . When Shabu pops out of the bottle, he's wearing a Bill Blass raw silk suit. You're not going to see me wearing a lot of jewelry and stuff."

The tempest subsided when *Just Our Luck* made its debut. Just its luck, it was scheduled opposite NBC's steamroller *The A-Team*, which *did* feature another actor "wearing a lot of jewelry and stuff." Faced with the competition of Mr. T, *Just Our Luck* folded within eleven episodes. Back in the bottle, fool!

Hogan's Heroes

CBS: 1965–1971

What a rollicking idea for a situation comedy—life among the prisoners of war in a German POW camp, complete with a laugh track to underscore the Nazi nuttiness. No one ever accused television programmers of having any sense of taste beyond their mouths, but *Hogan's Heroes* brought a new, appalling low to an industry that had already shown time and time again that when it came to making money, it had no shame.

Was CBS underestimating the American public? Not a chance, sorry to say: *Hogan's Heroes* ran for a mammoth total of 168 half-hour episodes on the network—two years longer than America was actually in the war. Heil Nielsens!

The idea for all the Gestapo giggles came from producer Ed Feldman. A play entitled *Stalag 17* had been a hit on Broadway in the 1950s, and a screen version with William Holden drew both critical plaudits and box-office bucks.

The only aspects of *Stalag 17* that apparently connected with Feldman were the bits of grim comedy that the POWs used to keep from going crazy. Sitcoms have been built on flimsier foundations than that, and the show was developed with the title *Hogan's Raiders*. At least they resisted the urge to call it *Führer Knows Best*.

For the title role of Colonel Robert Hogan, Feldman contacted Bob Crane, popular L.A. disc jockey and next-door neighbor on *The Donna Reed Show*. The king of the L.A. airwaves had managed to hold both jobs for two years, and he was looking for a property that would establish him as top banana.

"A comedy about a POW camp?" said Crane, after he had signed the contract for the show. "But then Eddie Feldman explained the plot to me. . . . So I thought, why not?"

There were any number of reasons why not, but from the beginning, Feldman, Desilu, and CBS went to great lengths to emphasize that

Bob Crane remained typecast as Colonel Hogan until his death in 1978. His body was discovered in an apartment, bludgeoned to death with a tire iron.

this was going to be a *tasteful* situation comedy about a POW camp, which might strike the average viewer as something like a *tasteful* situation comedy about a merry band of child molesters.

"It's halfway between *Combat* and *McHale's Navy*—with a little bit of *The Man from U.N.C.L.E.* thrown in," insisted Crane.

Werner Klemperer, who played the cartoonish Colonel Klink, was no stranger to playing Nazis in film and television; his Teutonic features and thick accent made him the ultimate American stereotype of the evil German soldier. His participation in *Hogan's Raiders* was doubly shocking—considering that the Klemperer family themselves fled the Nazis in the early 1930s.

John Banner played Sgt. Schultz, the corpulent *dummkopf* who kept repeating, "I zee nusssing, Colonel Hogan . . . nusssing. . . ." Banner had left Austria to escape the Nazis, and he didn't have a problem with the plot of *Hogan's Raiders*, "just so people don't get prisoner-of-war camps mixed up with concentration camps. You can't make fun of a concentration camp."

With this dubious distinction in mind, and the new title *Hogan's Heroes*, the show made CBS's fall schedule for 1965. Among the polyglot characters behind the barbed wire were a natty, resourceful Brit, played by future *Family Feud* host Richard Dawson; a tiny Frenchman, *Days of Our Lives* star Robert Clary; and a black corporal, played by future television director Ivan Dixon. There was also a blonde secretary on the Deutschland side, whose Hildegarde braids and mammoth bust made her look like the star of a drag opera.

This outrageous stereotyping made the show seem like a stalag adaptation of *Amos 'n Andy*, but that didn't seem to bother Feldman or the network; after all, if they could try to wring laughs out of Nazi Germany, any other sins were small potatoes. A minor flap *was* stirred, though, when humorist Stan Freberg was commissioned to make a radio commercial for the new show. Its tag line: "If you liked World War II, you'll *love* *Hogan's Heroes!*" Considering Freberg's sense of humor, the line was probably his commentary on the staggering bad taste of the operation, but CBS pulled the spot after some adverse publicity.

CBS enlisted Bob Crane as Johnny-on-the-spot to defend the program. "Depicting life in a German POW camp circa 1942 isn't the most ideal setting for a situation comedy," he conceded, insisting that "ex-POWs are our greatest boosters."

Crane, whose character was described in official network publicity as the "glib and impudent ringleader of a zany band of Allied captives in a German prisoner-of-war camp," also said, "We work hard on the scripts so the lines don't sound too jokey. In other words, we try to give *Hogan's*

Those naughty Nazis were always befuddled by wily Bob Crane in *Hogan's Heroes,* the only sitcom ever set in a German stalag. Ivan Dixon looks on.

Colonel Klink gets a rubdown from Colonel Hogan in another episode of *Hogan's Heroes*.

the extra thought which makes *The Dick Van Dyke Show*, for instance, so beautiful." Ed Feldman readily admitted that the writing staff used William Shirer's classic *The Rise and Fall of the Third Reich* as an inspiration for source material, lest anyone think that *Hogan's Heroes* was less than authentic.

That sort of care, beauty, and regard for propriety was evident in one publicity stunt that CBS cooked up for *Hogan's Heroes*. It was a cast and press party held at the Ocotillo Lodge in Palm Springs, California. The lodge had been cosmetically transformed into a festive replica of a POW camp. Blackshirted "guards" strutted their stuff to the sound of Deutschland military marches. Best of all, an actor costumed as Adolf Hitler even made an appearance— drunk. The only thing missing was a group of manacled CBS executives sporting yellow stars and pink triangles on their pinstriped suits.

Hogan's Heroes did produce one strange phenomenon: It managed to unite Jews, Germans, and the American Nazi Party, who all agreed that the show was one of the major embarrassments ever to be aired. Jews, of course, had no reason to laugh. For their part, Germans resented the monocle-and-jackboot stereotypes. And the American Nazi Party, surprisingly, thought that CBS was making a travesty of their plans for a Fourth Reich. Even with these disparate groups united against Hogan's

motley crew, the program was the ninth most popular program of the 1965–66 TV season, and the sixth most popular on the CBS network alone.

When it left the air after six years of decent ratings, *Hogan's Heroes* proved to be one of the most successful syndicated shows of all time. In 1972, it was running in *every* major U.S. city, as well as 45 different countries.

"We even tried to peddle it in West Germany!" said Werner Klemperer. "We got a 'no.'"

The most macabre twist to the *Hogan's Heroes* affair came on June 29, 1978. While in town for a dinner theater stint in Scottsdale, Arizona, Bob Crane was found murdered in his room. The killing was particularly brutal: two blows from a jack handle finished off the star while he lay in bed, and a cord from a nearby video camera had been tightened around his neck to ensure that the job had been thorough.

Although the police questioned family and friends, one of the earliest suspects was an American Nazi; the ritualistic nature of the murder led investigators to wonder whether an angry Nazi or group of Nazis had murdered Crane for revenge. This line of questioning, however, was quickly dismissed when an investigation of the actor's personal effects unearthed "dozens" of homemade videotapes featuring Crane in a variety of sex scenes. The pornography angle soon became more paramount to the case than any suspected Nazi angle, and the investigators indicted a video-equipment dealer from California. He was later released, and, to date, the case has never been solved.

"I'm not Joe Buffoon," Crane had insisted. "The lines have to mean something." To many people in America, the lines meant harmless laughs. To others, *Hogan's Heroes* was no joking matter—perhaps the greatest prime-time travesty of all.

Battles of the Sexes:
Men and Women Slug It Out for Fun and Prizes

A good screaming match between a man and a woman is one of the oldest and most satisfying forms of entertainment; just ask any city dweller who's ever spent an evening listening to a particularly juicy fight in the next apartment.

This battle primeval has also provided the basis for many wretched television programs. Since the dawn of the small screen, wily programmers have known that a nor-mally placid couple will gladly air their dirty laundry and checkered sexual histories to God and America—as long as there's the possibility that they might win a bedroom set, a microwave oven, or a year's supply of Rice-A-Roni.

Channel 4 is broadcasting some of the most outrageous examples of this peculiar brand of Love, American Style.

The Dating Game

ABC & SYNDICATED:
1965–1974, 1977–1980, 1985–

Anthropologists studying the evolution of the great American single need look no farther than the twenty-plus years of *The Dating Game*. It's the complete Fern Bar culture in a videotape nutshell, from the early days of ironed hair and miniskirts, through the what's-your-sign seventies, ending up at the thin leather ties and spiky haircuts on the neo-yuppies who populated the show during the eighties.

The Dating Game was Chuck Barris's first big success—the show that made all his future efforts, including *The Newlywed Game*, *The $1.98 Beauty Show*, and *The Gong Show* possible. The rules were simple: A beautiful "bachelorette" asks sexually suggestive questions of three horny bachelors, who are all shielded from view behind a partition. After a few rounds of sniggering banter ("Bachelor Number One: I play the trombone. If I played you, what would it sound like?"), the lissome miss picks one of the men for a vacation date. The gentlefolk then

depart on their dream date—sometimes to places as prosaic as San Diego or Lake Tahoe, sometimes to Austria or London—and everyone gathers at the end of the telecast to throw a kiss to the home audience, like a bunch of Dinah Shores with gold chains and chest hair.

In 1965, when the country was still more comfortable with George Burns than George Carlin, the prehistoric sexual humor of *The Dating Game* was still considered deliciously naughty, like one of those old Redd Foxx party albums conspicuously marked ADULTS ONLY. And, in fact, Barris found that contestants plunged into their roles as taste-violators with an abandon heretofore unseen on American TV. The first two weeks of production on the show resulted in hours of totally unusable tape. Examples:

Q: Bachelor Number One, one of my biggest difficulties is spelling. How do you spell relief?

A: F-A-R-T.

Q: Bachelor Number Three, what's the funniest thing you were ever caught doing when you thought nobody was looking?

A: I was caught with a necktie around my dick.

Q: Bachelor Number Two, what would I like most about you?

A: My cock.

Yes. Well. Harrumph. Barris and company were quickly sent scrambling to produce shows that contained sexual innuendo—and innuendo only, as the ABC censors were, for some reason, turning into a bunch of party poopers. The problem was solved by hiring an actor who posed as an agent from the FCC, who addressed the contestants before the show and told them in no uncertain terms that references to stiff anatomy would result in stiff fines and jail terms. After this caveat was introduced, the tapings calmed down and settled at the level of adolescent T & A humor that would make the show so enduringly popular on daytime TV. (A prime-time *Dating Game* was a hit for over three years on ABC.)

When the program left the network, it continued to be popular in syndication with all its tacky hallmarks intact: the pop-psychedelic set, the obligatory kiss that signed the show off, and hosting by "Gentleman" Jim Lange, a disc jockey who presided for fifteen years in his ruffled shirts and Tijuana-rental tuxes.

Saturday Night Live effectively lampooned the show with a sketch called "The Dating Zone," which featured Bob Newhart as an unwilling househusband dragged into a TV studio to ask questions like "Bachelorette Number Three: If I was doing a crossword puzzle and needed a five-letter word for 'cat' beginning with 'P' and ending with 'Y'. . ."

It looked like the televised mating ritual had come to an end in 1980, when *The Dating Game* ceased production and began the rerun circuit—giving home viewers the chance to watch a beautiful woman blow her chance to date an "unknown bachelor" named Tom Selleck, as well as other stars who had trod the dating boards in search of some exposure and a free trip.

In TV, though, you can't keep a bad thing down, and the syndicated success of *The New Newlywed Game* in 1985 led to *The New Dating Game* in 1986. In a blow for equal rights, "Gentleman" Jim Lange and his cheesy tuxedos were gone, replaced by perky Elaine Joyce—perennial game-show panelist and star of such worthy features as *Motel Hell*. If nothing else, Joyce proved that a female game show host could be just as fawning and fatuous as a male. She even had a mysterious New Age sign-off as arcane as Dan Rather's "Courage!"; at the end of each telecast, she looked into the camera and told the audience, "Straight ahead."

The success of this new version

must have given Chuck Barris heart, and perhaps an idea or two for still another program detailing the battle of the sexes (or sexless, as the case may be). With the marital breakup rate spiraling every year, why not *The Divorce Game*? Its first competitors, of course, would be couples who met on *The Dating Game*, married, and subsequently split up over their mismatched answers on *The Newlywed Game*. With special celebrity guests ranging from Zsa Zsa Gabor to Mickey Rooney, that old sly boots Chuck Barris might find his despicable duo of game shows turned into a terrible trilogy.

The Newlywed Game

ABC: 1966–1974
SYNDICATED: 1977–1980, 1984–

"Fill in the blank," says Bob Eubanks. "My husband is a closet . . . what?"

The heavy, sixtyish woman obviously doesn't understand the question. She looks out into the audience while her brow furrows. The host waits. She thinks for a long moment, and finally comes up with a tentative, desperate answer.

"Queen?"

Ah, those crazy newlyweds— eight of them per show, five shows per week, for 20 years and, no doubt, a long time into the future. Why, you put a fellow and his gal in front of those cameras, and you just don't know what they might say. Like the time that Bob Eubanks asked a couple about their most unusual "whoopee session," a whoopee session worthy of *The Wacky World of Whoopee* magazine. One young woman thought about the question seriously before answering how it had to be the time her husband tied her to the bed before getting bored with the whole thing; he then re-treated to the living room to watch television. "I think it was *The New Love American Style* on TV," she recounted to the nonplussed Eubanks.

That's the story and the glory of love on *The Newlywed Game*, the show that proved to be producer Chuck Barris's most enduring success. It began on ABC as a daytime offering in July 1966, and was so popular that a prime-time version was added six months later. The nighttime edition ran for 4½ seasons—a hit by any standards—and the daytime show lasted for 8½ years on the network before going into reruns and syndication. For the last 20 years, *The Newlywed Game* has been a regular staple of American television, presided over in every edition by the smirkingly handsome Bob Eubanks.

Like all runaway TV successes, the premise of *Newlywed* was simplicity itself. Four couples competed by trying to match answers; the wives were asked a series of questions while the husbands were out of earshot. When the husbands returned, they tried to match answers with their spouses to earn points. In the other half of the show, the situation was reversed, and the show concluded with the awarding of an inexpensive prize—kitchen appliances or a dinette—to the winning couple.

It would have been just as easy to persuade a Cadillac dealer, for example, to donate the gifts for such a remarkably successful show, but Chuck Barris himself put the kibosh on that idea. "We couldn't make the prizes too luxurious; when we did, the program turned violent. . . . We upgraded our prizes once for a few weeks—with disastrous results," he recalled in his autobiography. "A missed answer would cause a couple to become dangerously pernicious. They would immediately lose their sense of humor and begin bashing each other on the head with their thick cardboard answer cards."

Ah, the answer cards, an integral part of any *Newlywed Game* telecast, and the element that at times made the contestants look like Punch and Judy. A wrong answer would often be cause for a mild case of husband-bashing or wife-beating with the offending answer card.

"Sure, the show caused some divorces," reasoned Chuck Barris. "Forty percent of our *Newlywed Game* couples, in fact, never celebrated their tenth anniversary. But then, neither did 40 percent of the rest of the country's married couples.

In any case, if a newlywed couple loved and respected each other, they probably would never have thought about doing the show in the first place. And even if they had, we would most likely not have selected them for the program. They would have made lousy contestants."

"What's the longest amount of time you've ever made your husband wait for . . . you-know-what?"

The contestant, Raynelle, reasons the question out. "Well, there's only one reason I ever make him wait," she says. "So it's got to be a week."

Bright contestants were also lousy contestants. After all, *The Newlywed Game* was hardly *Jeopardy!;* knowledge of "Biblical Characters" or "Potent Potables" got you nowhere with Bob Eubanks. The questions were divided into several rough categories:

Silly questions. These were bizarre, hypothetical queries, sometimes with a vaguely insulting edge. "Fill in the blank: 'My wife's brain is the size of . . . what?" or "Will your wife say her mouth could or could not hold an entire Quarter Pounder . . . with cheese?"

Friends and family questions. These questions often impugned a mother-in-law, or forced a man to name the ugliest of his wife's pals.

On one telecast, when Eubanks asked a woman to name the one thing that her mother didn't particularly like about her husband, the wife squirmed and conceded, "My mother doesn't really like him. I wish you wouldn't ask this."

Dumdum questions. The humor here stemmed from the couples' ignorance of etymology or geography. When Eubanks asked four California couples to name the foreign country closest to their front door, he received answers like "Our house faces west, so it's got to be Japan" and "Definitely Hawaii."

In an interview, Eubanks recalled that one woman thought her husband's favorite rodent was a saxophone, and noted that the definition of the word "masticate" often tripped up unwary couples.

"Whoopee" questions. "Whoopee" was the show's censor-sanctioned euphemism for sex, and it made for many a merry question: "Not counting your wife, who's the first person that comes to mind when you close your eyes and think of whoopee?" or "When you and your husband first made whoopee, was he a limp shrimp, a stout trout, or a virgin sturgeon?"

These mini-peeks into the petty squabbles and equally petty boudoirs of *Newlywed* contestants made the show an instant hit when it debuted as a companion piece to the successful *Dating Game* in 1966. Each show began with an announcer intoning, "Heeeeere come the newlyweds!," as four couples in four trellis-bedecked love seats rolled out onstage in front of a cheesy gazebo set. From then on in, it was ritual humiliation for the couples; the losers were kept discreetly out of camera range while the winners smooched and embraced at the sight of their new dishwasher or television set.

As it would be throughout its run, the show was hosted by Los Angeles disc jockey Bob Eubanks, whose career had received a large boost when he spotted an obscure British rock group called the Beatles and successfully promoted their first West Coast concert at the Hollywood Bowl. From there, it was a hop, a snigger, and a jump to becoming the host of *Newlywed*, occasionally moonlighting to host short-lived game shows like *Diamond Head, Rhyme or Reason,* and *Trivia Trap.*

The shock-and-smirk approach proved durable for quite a while. Even though ABC first removed the show from its nighttime schedule, and then from its daytime lineup (where its Felliniesque view of suburbia more properly belonged), Barris continued to syndicate the show through the end of the 1970s, with the same mock-romantic set, the same Vegasy music, and the same repartee from old smoothie Bob Eubanks. If it wasn't for the width of Eubanks' ties and sideburns changing every so often, it could have been one episode played over and over again, *ad nauseam*. Its last gasp came in 1980, but the seventies reruns continued to play on independent stations in syndication throughout the eighties.

But the 1970s was the decade that shockproofed America, beginning with Archie Bunker and ending with the calculated outrages of *Soap* and *Mary Hartman, Mary Hartman*. Clearly a success like *The Newlywed Game* couldn't remain dormant for long.

Sure enough; fans of schlock television thrilled to the news that *The New Newlywed Game* would be returning to American living rooms in the fall of 1985. The astronomical ratings of *Wheel of Fortune* had sent producers scrambling for game shows that could be scheduled during the dinner hour (6:30 to 8 P.M.) as an alternative to network news.

Any changes in the *New Newlywed Game* were purely cosmetic. Instead of a plastic bower, the new newlyweds conducted their cardbashing in what looked like a pastel Pachinko machine, augmented by modern electronic effects. Silhouettes of arguing spouses served as a backdrop. Still in place, though, were Bob Eubanks, the comparatively cheap grand prizes, and, of course, the thick answer cards. *TV Guide* was impressed enough to laud the show as "the worst piece of sleaze on television today"—no small accolade.

A visit to the set of *The New Newlywed Game* revealed another change, though. In keeping with the times, the questions had gotten progressively nastier, more explicit, and more geared to personal matters. While there were still the innocently inane queries here and there ("Will your husband say that most of his jackets zip, snap, or button?"), there was an increase in the number of "naughty" questions, the kind that kept the studio audience giggling nervously and the censors on the edge of their seats. "Boobs" and "buns" had replaced the more chaste "chest" and "derriere", and the insults were flying even more frequently. Also in keeping with the societal changes between 1966 and 1986, the couples were younger, often looking as if they were at the end of their teens.

One question seemed to flummox that day's panelists: "When it comes to the team of love, is your husband playing in the major leagues, the little leagues . . . or is he on the farm team?"

Obviously trying to compliment her husband, one young woman shook her head confidently and said, "Oh, the farm team! He's an animal!"

Her husband was equally confident of his own prowess, but he had more knowledge of sports terms and told Eubanks that he was in the majors. In the subsequent uproar over the correct answer, his wife became even more flummoxed and managed to stammer, "I told them you were into animals!"

The audience howled.

Nothing in the rest of the taping could top *that*, although Eubanks got the fellows going by asking about "the most indecent outfit she owns." The responses included "a red thing with a hole in the back," "a Frederick's of Hollywood nightgown," and "crotchless panties." (That last item of lingerie was bleeped, and it appeared on the answer card as "incomplete panties.")

Still, the sixteen contestants on that day's taping seemed jubilant, a little embarrassed, and none the worse for wear after the taping. And that seems to be what keeps Chuck Barris Productions in forty newlyweds a week for each version of the show; the appeal of appearing on national television and possibly winning a prize is as strong a lure as it was back in 1955, when a woman would detail the gory miseries of her life on TV just for the chance to be named *Queen for a Day*.

But even the potential promise of a living room set skirts the question of why thousands of people line up for this kind of treatment. Chuck Barris, one of the wisest if most tasteless purveyors of pop entertainment, proved that it wasn't the prizes when he made *The $1.98 Beauty Show* a hit. Even the promise of less than two dollars and a bouquet of wilted greens wasn't the bait. The bait was television itself. As Chuck Barris himself said, "Their memories of show biz—with all its glamorous and narcissistic trappings—were ample reward."

3's a Crowd

SYNDICATED: 1979–1980

"Who knows a man best . . . his wife, or his *secretary*??!!"

That was the gimmick behind *3's a Crowd*, a short-lived show that took the premise of *The Newlywed Game* and added the husband's secretary to the whole mess. Only 105 episodes were ever taped, but during that time, *3's a Crowd* was rarely out of the public eye.

Veteran TV watchers might guess that the hand of Chuck Barris was responsible for stroking this flaccid excuse for entertainment. They'd be right. *Crowd* came along at a time when Barris could do no wrong, with *The Gong Show*, *The $1.98 Beauty Show*, and other sadomasochistic game shows cleaning up in the ratings.

Like *Newlywed*, *Dating*, and the other Barris games, the premise of *Crowd* was simple. It was created back in 1967, when it was considered too offensive to succeed, but the successes of Barris's latter-day efforts must have made the crew at Chuck Barris Productions a bit heady.

It was essentially a retread of *The Newlywed Game*, with three rounds. First, the hubbies answered a series of questions that were, if anything, more embarrassing than those on *Newlywed:*

"What's the main reason your secretary should go braless?"

"If you and your secretary decided to make whoopee in the office, what would be the most inventive place you could think of?"

"My wife *blanks* like a man. Fill in the blank."

"How much would one night with your secretary be worth to you?"

And so it went. After the husbands answered all the questions, the wives would be called back onstage to supply their answers, and awarded points for each one that matched their husbands'. In the final portion of the show, the secretaries would do the same. Rolling pins were not supplied for use on the gentlemen's skulls, but the stiff white cards upon which the answers were written proved to be equally effective.

The grand prize on the show was a meager thousand dollars, and it didn't end up in the hands of the winning husband-wife-secretary triumvirate, but was instead split among all the wives or all the secretaries, depending on which team had the highest score. The fellows were merely sent home with a selection of what TV euphemistically calls "lovely parting gifts"—and the satisfaction, no doubt, of thinking themselves to have appeared rather studly on national television.

With the confidence of seasoned pros, Barris and longtime producer Michael Metzger (who began working for Barris back in 1966) started *3's a Crowd* as both a daytime *and* nighttime entry, instead of taking the more prudent route of waiting to see if the daily show would snigger its way into a hit. Operating on the wisdom that low concepts produced high ratings, 140 television markets signed on to carry the show—a new television record. Even more astoundingly, all this was achieved without a pilot.

This latest show, though, was different. Women across America had had enough. When groups like Los Angeles Working Women and the National Organization for Women began raising a hue and cry, the Barris company must have thought that it was just more good publicity. Wrong, Chuckie Baby.

Producer Michael Metzger defended *3's a Crowd* by appealing to viewers' tastes, as if the producers had merely aired an episode of *Masterpiece Theatre* with a few racy words. "With our show, as in a good movie where the characters have been developed, you get to know the people," he informed the press. "It's kind of a *real* drama with *real* people.

"A vast majority of businesses contain these triangle situations. I find it incredibly interesting. People seem to recognize the fact that there's a certain amount of rivalry between the wife and the secretary, and they seem to come on the show with the expectation that they'll get into trouble.

"It's a kind of therapy."

Therapy? Certainly anyone interested in appearing on *3's a Crowd* should have had his or her head examined. But the controversy didn't have long to continue. First, in Detroit (where *3's a Crowd* beat all the competition in its 7:30 time slot), a protest from the United Auto Workers women's committee had the show hastily withdrawn from the air. And when the National Organization for Women drew *Crowd* into its sights, more stations began dropping the show.

Caving in to station defection and public protest, *3's a Crowd* was withdrawn from production after one year and only 105 shows—well before the fun-loving staff at Barris Productions could begin the jokes about stenographers who use their boss's Dictaphone.

Sick Transit:
The Auto-erotic Shows About Cars and Trains

A TV character's mode of transportation has always said a lot about him—ever since Gene Autry rode Champion down the tube in 1947.

Adam "Batman" West had his trusty Batmobile. Don Johnson would have found it tough to track down Miami's drug trade in a VW Rabbit rather than a Testarossa. And let's not forget Gavin MacLeod, who would have been high and dry without *The Love Boat*.

But some hapless TV types would have done better to stick to their own two feet. Now showing on Channel 5 are some of the, well, more *special* relationships between men and their machines.

My Mother the Car

NBC: 1965–1966

"Dick was the good boy and I was the bad," said the hapless Jerry Van Dyke in a burst of candor. "No matter how well I did things, Dick could always do them five times better. I always came out the loser. Like even today, my press clippings have headlines like 'My Brother, the Star.'"

My Brother, the Star might have been an intriguing premise for a situation comedy: a story about a frustrated sibling, always forced into the role of second banana to Big Brother. Unfortunately, Jerry Van Dyke had to live that role in real life; on television, he was the star of *My Mother the Car*—a program that put the boob in the boob tube.

The man doomed to fame as "Dick's brother" came to Hollywood with hopes of scoring big. After leaving Danville, Illinois, the elder Van Dyke had his own eponymous situation comedy on CBS, lauded by critics and audiences alike as an intelligently written, funny show. He'd even had motion picture success with

Bye Bye Birdie and *Mary Poppins*.

It all must have seemed terribly tantalizing to Jerry, who had become a celebrity of sorts in Terre Haute, Indiana, as the host of a local talk show. His first national break came on his brother's program; Dick had related a tale about Jerry's sleep-walking habits in a *Dick Van Dyke Show* script meeting, and the writers thought it good enough to commission a script about it. When it came time to film the episode, Dick recommended Jerry for the part, and thus began Jerry's recurring role as Stacey Petrie on *The Dick Van Dyke Show*. Watching the look-alike brothers play off each other gave CBS an idea. If one Van Dyke was good, two Van Dykes would be terrific.

The network quickly signed Little Brother to a two-year contract amid much fanfare, proclaiming, "Jerry Van Dyke is a marvelously fresh talent who, with seasoning, will be a big star."

His seasoning, roasting, and basting began with *Picture This*, a

Jerry Van Dyke charmed Rose Marie on one of his *Dick Van Dyke Show* appearances, but his greatest fame was to come a year or two later as the star of *My Mother the Car*.

comedy game show that debuted on the network as a summer replacement in 1963. Contestants had to do sketches to win money. *TV Guide* described the show as "inane"; Jerry preferred the adjective "terrible." By the end of the summer, *Picture This* was out of the picture.

The network decided that their newest hot commodity might attain fame as a song-and-dance comedian, à la Dick. He was plopped into the role of Judy Garland's sidekick on *The Judy Garland Show*—a variety program for which CBS held the highest of expectations. Jerry's biggest running gag was a kidding insult—"What's an old lady like you doing on television?"—that didn't endear him to Garland fans.

Producers George Schlatter and Norman Jewison both left before the show was three months old, and the third producer saw fit to can Jerry Van Dyke in an attempt to salvage Garland's reputation. That ended Van Dyke's CBS "seasoning."

"The only break I ever had was that no one watched it," he said of *The Judy Garland Show,* no doubt wishing that he could click his heels together three times and erase the whole experience.

NBC was willing to give Jerry Van Dyke a shot with a new concept that had been cooked up by producer/writer/director Rod Amateau. It was the story of a small-town lawyer and family man who discovers that his late mother has been reincarnated in the person of a vintage automobile—a concept farther out on a limb than Shirley MacLaine.

(Largely forgotten now is the name of another of *My Mother the Car*'s writer-creators: Allan Burns. Burns escaped *My Mother* unscathed, going on in the seventies to industry laurels by creating *The Mary Tyler Moore Show* and *Lou Grant*.)

Van Dyke thanked NBC for giving him his first chance to "be myself," although he spent much of the summer of 1965 defending the show against snickering journalists and their poisonous pens, which were slamming the show even before its debut. "It's not a story about a car, but about a guy's problems and situations. Every now and then my mother helps me out with a problem," Van Dyke explained, as if *My Mother the Car* was merely a sitcom version of *Psycho*, with himself in the Tony Perkins role.

"Mother" was played by two people—or rather, one person and one car. NBC customized an antique flivver, christening it "a 1928 Porter" for the show (despite the fact that a "Porter" never existed). For the voice of "Mom," unheard by anyone but her sonnyboy, NBC tested Eve Arden and Jean Arthur before settling on Ann Sothern of *Private Secretary* fame, who had lately found herself doing summer stock theater and playing slattern roles in pictures like *Lady in a Cage*.

Asked why she was supplying

the voice of a talking car, becoming the distaff version of Chill Wills on *Mr. Ed*, Sothern replied honestly, "I am interested in money. Anyway, I'm an actress and I want to act. I don't want to sit around waiting for the great things that never come along."

Jerry Van Dyke still preferred to think of *My Mother the Car* in terms more rosy than the show might have deserved. "What we are doing is situation comedy with a gimmick. We don't want to overdo the gimmick, to use the car any more than we have to. . . . The situation may be nutty, but I will be real.

"All you have to believe is that the car is my mother."

Yup.

The show's establishing episode began with Van Dyke, as Jerry Crabtree, shopping for a used station wagon that would accommodate his happy suburban family—doting wife and precocious kids. While in a used-car lot, though, an auto door "magically" opens by itself, smacking him in the derriere. "Hello, son," the radio blares in Ann Sothern's voice, and the hilarity is launched.

The Porter proved to have the personality of a nagging Jewish mother, demanding everything but chicken soup in her (its?) gas tank. Like *Mr. Ed*, Mother, fearing installation in the Smithsonian, wouldn't speak to anyone but her son, which supposedly kept the yuks rolling as well.

Crabtree's wife, Barbara, and the kids all loathed the clunky old car, and kept badgering poor Dave for a shiny new wood-paneled station wagon. Mom proved to be a pain as well, needing her hood shined up for a night on the town or demanding a television set installed in the garage.

The villain of the show was mustachioed Avery Schreiber as Captain Mancini, an autophile who spent his time scheming to buy—or steal—Mother. Whenever Mom sounded the alert with her antique horn, the baddies would be scared off.

It's unlikely that Sir Laurence Olivier could have overcome material like that, and it was a sure bet that Jerry Van Dyke wasn't able to make comedic history when Mother developed "carthritis" or boiled over in a fit of Porter pique. One episode even went so far as to make fun of drunk driving; Mother got tipsy on antifreeze and Crabtree, behind the wheel, was pulled over.

Unlike Van Dyke, Sothern could comfort herself with the knowledge that she was never seen on camera. Her lines were originally dubbed into the film while she watched each episode, but soon she didn't even have to watch; the producers simply had the veteran star record her lines while reading directly from the script. (It took three or four hours a week to play Mother—doing two or three episodes at a time.) "I play her as a pretty hip character," said Sothern, explaining her Stanislavskian motivations, "although so far I must

Oedipus Wreck: Jerry Van Dyke tries to get out of an awkward situation with his wife, Maggie Pierce, on *My Mother the Car*. Mom's "head" is visible in the foreground. *NBC*

admit my dialogue hasn't been earth-shattering."

One person did like the show, however: Dr. Charles Ansell, president of the L.A. Society of Clinical Psychologists, saw *My Mother the Car* as a modern retelling of *Oedipus Rex*. Sophocles might have had a seizure, but Dr. Ansell referred to the program as "a gold mine of psychoanalytic insights, unintended by the producers, but guided by that buried part of the infantile mind which still lives on in their adult mentality."

Ansell got the infantile-mind part right, but he might have revealed more about himself than about Freud when he expostulated on even deeper meanings within the scripts of *My Mother the Car*.

"Jerry Van Dyke acts out every man's basic dream," proclaimed the good doctor, "to conquer the mother and have her for himself. Jerry is in complete possession of his car/mother. She is powerless when he locks the garage door."

Dr. Ansell, by the way, also happened to be Jerry Van Dyke's personal psychologist, which must have been handy when the network yanked *My Mother the Car* from its schedule. After all, without such an understanding shrink, Van Dyke might have gone the true Oedipal route and poked his eyes out.

Support from the Ovaltine generation wasn't enough to rescue *Mother* and son. Its macho competition, *Combat* and *Rawhide*, quickly ground Dave Crabtree and his long-suffering mama into the dust, and the brickbats that assailed the show all season ensured that *My Mother the Car* wouldn't be back for a second year.

Shortly after the cancellation, Van Dyke changed his tune as to the purported quality of the deceased program. "When I landed that TV series," he said, "my wife and I were happy. We were going to settle down for the first time in our lives. Boy, it was worse than all our years on the road.

"I was unhappy about the scripts, but I found out that when you take a series, that's it. You have no say about anything. You're just the guy who catches the blame when the show folds. . . . I can make just as much money in Las Vegas and around the country. I gotta be careful now. Believe me, from now on, I'm going to like the script."

Van Dyke went on to other careers, each with about the same success as *My Mother the Car*. He starred in several other undistinguished shows like *Accidental Family* and *The Headmaster*. (Despite the title of the latter show, his costar was Andy Griffith, not Linda Lovelace.)

Van Dyke resurfaced briefly as the star of a 1979 ABC comedy, *13 Queens Boulevard* (seven episodes), before forsaking the TV grind to open his own nitery in the San Fernando Valley. "Jerry Van Dyke's Supper Club" never quite caught on among

After the debacle of *My Mother the Car*, Jerry Van Dyke went on to star with Andy Griffith in *Headmaster*.

Angelenos to become the Valley version of Spago or Chasen's, although Van Dyke did attract such name talent as Pat Buttram from *Green Acres*. *Fresno*, the comedy miniseries in which he costarred with Carol Burnett, didn't make a dent in the Nielsens.

Even after 25 years of hard work in Hollywood, poor Jerry Van Dyke is still best known as "Dick's brother,"

and it may ever be thus. And, as always, Dick Van Dyke has the last word:

"Jerry and I were talking the other day," said the elder Van Dyke, "about who has the biggest closet of pilots that never sold. Of course, I was able to do mine in relative obscurity. Unfortunately for Jerry, his bombs were all in the glare of publicity."

Supertrain

NBC: 1979

Pity poor NBC. At the end of the 1970s, the third-rated network was flopping around like Orca, the killer whale, in a wading pool, continually beaching itself with half-baked programs that lasted less than six weeks, if they (and the viewers) were lucky.

Consider the dishonor roll from this era at NBC: *Hello, Larry; Grandpa Goes to Washington; The Misadventures of Sheriff Lobo; Pink Lady and Jeff; Turnabout.* These shows were about, respectively: McLean Stevenson; a lovable old coot who becomes a senator; a bumbling Southern sheriff; two non-English-speaking Japanese pop stars; and a man and a woman who wake up one morning to find that their personalities have changed bodies.

Still, these shows seemed positively Shakespearean compared to the muddle that was *Supertrain,* a *Love Boat* rip-off that cost the network upward of $10 million (though the precise figures aren't readily available) and lasted less than six months on the NBC schedule. It also

sank the career of Fred Silverman. Two years after the failure of *Supertrain,* Silverman became the Man Without a Network, and the failure of his gold-plated choochoo led cynics to suspect that Silverman was secretly on the payroll of one of the competing networks, being paid to turn the National Broadcasting Company into a National Basket Case.

Having already catapulted CBS and ABC successively into the Number One networks by the mid-seventies, there were only two places left for Silverman to set his sights. PBS might have benefited from Silverman's golden touch, but to NBC he went, where he began to cannibalize his own spoor with a *Love Boat* rip-off so blatant that ABC might have had grounds for legal action had *Supertrain* been a hit. We're certain it was all a coincidence, of course, but the facts remain. Consider:

Love Boat had a Balding, Silvery-haired Patriarch as the ship's captain; *Supertrain* had a Balding,

Any resemblance to *The Love Boat* was purely intentional. Joey Aresco, Ilene Graff, and George Boone were among the staff on the doomed *Supertrain,* a Titanic on wheels. *NBC*

Silvery-haired Patriarch as the train's conductor.

The Ship had a Doctor played by Bernie Kopell, so the Train had to have a Doctor—played by Robert Alda.

The startling departure, however, came in the casting of a bartender. On *Love Boat*, a Low-key, Wisecracking Black Guy poured the drinks, while on *Supertrain* the mixologist was most definitely white. Just to cover his bets, however, Silverman did have a Low-key Wisecracking Black Guy with an amazing resemblance to *Love Boat*'s Ted Lange. He played the porter, which must have delighted the NAACP.

These people were merely third bananas, though, to the real star: Supertrain itself, which seemed to be a cross between a Japanese bullet train and a Ferrari Testarossa. It lapped the miles at incredible speed, and was almost a self-contained city, complete with *Love Boat*-borrowed accoutrements like restaurants, a gymnasium, and, best of all, a heated swimming pool. Amtrak, eat your heart out.

NBC threw its complete weight behind *Supertrain*, as did Silverman himself, and the combined girths were not inconsiderable. The new president thought that the train was super enough to pull the entire network out of the gutter, and he planned to use it as the linchpin for his entire lineup. It became imperative to get the show on the air ASAP;

if that meant building sets and train models without minor technicalities like finished blueprints, so be it.

Dan Curtis, the producer of *Supertrain*, recalled the chaos. "I told him [Silverman] there was no way to get this show on the air when he wanted it, but I got the message from him that cost was no object—just get it on the air."

That attitude became a selling point in NBC's publicity blitz surrounding the show. Many Americans began hearing about *Supertrain* months before it was to make its debut in February 1979. Much was made of the elaborate Godzilla-style miniatures of the train itself, a ploy apparently designed to appeal to the millions of American men who had HO-gauge trains in their basements.

A full-sized model of the train had been built (occupying three large soundstages), but shots of Supertrain's nine behemoth cars roaring through the countryside were obviously going to have to be done in miniature. A 1½″ scale model was built, as was a ¾″ model.

In addition, crews were kept busy concocting tiny landscapes for the trains to drive through while the passengers inside did the latest *Saturday Night Fever* steps in the train disco or lounged around the not-quite-Olympic-sized train pool.

By February, things were ready, even if *Supertrain* was held together with spit, baling wire, and guest stars of dubious luminosity. Where

"All aboard for fun," said the caption on this priceless shot. Smiling *Love Boat* veterans Zsa Zsa Gabor and Lyle Waggoner were among the guests on the first episode of the new and improved *Supertrain. NBC*

ABC merely had a dinky dinghy bumping around the ocean, NBC had a brawny, powerful cross-country choochoo. Where ABC only had five "regulars" as the *Love Boat* crew, NBC had ten on its *Supertrain*.

The network was so confident of the show's success that it scheduled *Supertrain* on Wednesday evenings at 8:00 opposite formidable competition: *Eight Is Enough* on ABC and *The Jeffersons* on CBS. The time slot had previously belonged to the umpteenth Dick Clark variety show, *Dick Clark's Live Wednesday*, which collapsed like a cheap facelift when confronted by George Jefferson.

Supertrain's debut drew hefty ratings. But by the second week, the audience defected en masse.

Sensing that something had gone drastically wrong, but unwilling to eat the investment they had made in the show so far, NBC executives pulled *Supertrain* from the schedule for repairs in early March. They fired all but three members of the cast—keeping the conductor, the doctor, and the porter—and gave the porter a new title, "Passenger Relations Officer." Since the cast now resembled the *Love Boat* crew more than ever, NBC went all the way and hired a Pert Blonde Social Director who had the same pixieish haircut as did the Pert Blonde Social Director on *Love Boat.*

Supertrain was even moved to Saturday nights in the 10:00–11:00 time slot, where, it was hoped, it would pick up the *Love Boat* audience when that show went off the air at 10:00. Billing it as "the all-new *Supertrain,*" NBC crossed its corporate fingers and hoped for a fresh start. The first all-new, lemon-freshened, better-than-ever episode featured veteran actors and familiar faces Zsa Zsa Gabor and Lyle Waggoner, who were no strangers to cruising on *The Love Boat* themselves.

Supertrain redebuted in April opposite ABC's own *Love Boat* rip-off, *Fantasy Island.* In the Battle of the Network Rip-offs, it was no contest. The *Island* scored a touchdown in the first quarter against *Supertrain.* By July, the all-new *Supertrain* was capturing only 19 percent of viewers watching TV during that time, and an embarrassed network began unhitching the cars and dismantling the locomotive.

Supertrain was not just another in NBC's long string of flops, however; the shock waves from its failure resonated throughout the network like fallout from the most atomic of TV bombs. This bomb thoroughly cooked the sizable caboose of Fred Silverman and his career at NBC.

Knight Rider

NBC: 1982–1986

Ah, the bonding that occurs between man and his car. Sigmund Freud would have a lot to say about Jerry Van Dyke's compulsion to keep Mom bright and shiny in *My Mother the Car*, and for more than a decade that bit of abnormal psychology was enough to keep America speculating about what *really* might have taken place during those cold nights in the garage.

Despite *Easy Rider*, television remained squeamish about exploring the psychosexual lengths that man would go to for machine—and vice versa—but in 1982 a program debuted that was even more shocking. The children for whom the show was ostensibly aimed saw *Knight Rider* as just another *Dukes of Hazzard*, an entertaining action show about a modern-day good guy and his trusty car, the contemporary equivalent of a cowboy and his horse. But adults must have been surprised to find *Knight Rider* a more subtle allegory about the love between a man and

his wheels. And, unlike *My Mother the Car*, this automobile was undeniably—shudder—another male!

That's right. Although the women tended to come and go in the life of Michael Knight (David Hasselhoff), the one constant in his life was his faithful Pontiac Trans-Am, a car so futuristic that it made the Batmobile look like a Model T. The car, KITT, even spoke, in slightly persnickety tones reminiscent of an irked drag queen. When series star Hasselhoff, clad in his characteristic Levis and flashing the whitest of smiles, would banter with KITT, the net effect was that of a Motor City version of La Car Aux Folles.

All this radical indoctrination couldn't possibly be presented on network television without some elaborate subterfuge. *Knight Rider* was ostensibly the story of Michael Knight, a former cop who became a crusading crimefighter after an "Eccentric Millionaire" died (Eccentric Millionaires are so popular with tele-

Zoom! David Hasselhoff demonstrates his racing prowess in this thrilling scene from *Knight Rider*.
Michael Jacobs Photojournalism

vision scriptwriters), leaving Knight in the possession of KITT. The Eccentric Millionaire, whose super-advanced factory had produced the vehicle, placed both Knight and the Trans-Am in the hands of a bachelor executor, Devon Miles (played by Edward Mulhare).

This hoary plot seemed cadged from several other series, including, but not limited to, *The Dukes of Hazzard. Knight Rider* also borrowed from *Batman*, in which an Eccentric Millionaire and "his young ward, Dick Grayson" fought crime in the superequipped Batmobile. Veteran TV viewers might also detect a whiff of *Magnum, P.I.* in this scenario—the sleuth show featured a handsome hunk who inherited the use of both a Ferrari and an uptight majordomo from an Eccentric Millionaire who lived in Hawaii. And like the shows that were its predecessors, on *Knight Rider* no woman ever intruded between two men and their car.

Upon its debut, critics and naysayers immediately sneered that the car was the best actor on the show, and that might not have been far from the truth; KITT's voice was supplied by veteran actor William Daniels, who later won an Emmy for his starring role on *St. Elsewhere*. Hasselhoff had little to do other than to banter with KITT and vanquish a baddie or two, but it was enough to qualify him for the Prime-Time Hall of Hunk Fame. At least KITT could fly—that is, when he and Knight weren't settling in for an evening of chitty-chitty-bang-bang.

The bond between man and machine didn't quite end on the set, either. Hasselhoff used to drive the distinctive black Trans-Am home at the end of every shooting day, but the result became confusion in the streets of Hollywood as fans began following the two back to Hasselhoff's home. The star soon took another Trans-Am with him instead (no doubt leaving KITT crying in his garage and swigging motor oil), but that proved unsatisfactory as well, so Hasselhoff regretfully took another make of car entirely. That did the trick, but it's unclear what Hasselhoff's real-life wife, actress Catherine Hickland, thought of her husband's strange fascination with KITT.

David Hasselhoff spoke of his nonhuman costar in glowing terms to the media as well. "When I first read the script," he said, "I thought it was a starmaker because it is a show about heroes—along the lines of Roy Rogers and Trigger or the Lone Ranger and Silver. When the car dies, I'm going to have it stuffed."

Their close bond didn't escape the marketing whizzes at Pontiac, who immediately hired the star to pitch Trans-Am automobiles at car shows. The result was an upsurge in Trans-Am sales—perhaps by lonely gentlemen seeking a little romance in their lives.

NBC tried introducing female interests into the show, but a woman never quite fit in when it came to *Knight Rider*'s all-male camaraderie. Actress Patricia McPherson originally played Bonnie, a curvaceous computer whiz who coddled KITT's intricate circuitry, but she was yanked after the first year and replaced by the even more buxom Rebecca Holden. After one year of the fiery-haired Holden tending to KITT and Michael's needs, the network gave up and re-replaced her with McPherson—but then, the course of true love ne'er did run smooth.

Eventually, the budding love affair began to flag in the ratings, and *Knight Rider* was quietly taken from the schedule after years of car chases, bionic feats, and weekly examples of *Road and Track* derring-do. To the end, however, the fourth-graders who constituted *Knight Rider*'s most loyal audience never caught on to the special relationship that existed between Michael and KITT, who remained faithful and true to each other. Scarlett and Rhett should have had such a happy ending.

Hello, I Must Be Going:
TV's One-Night Stands and Short-Lived Shows

Even the most threadbare of television programs requires a substantial cash outlay just to get the first episode on the air. Staffs, cast, and crew must all be hired; a set has to be built; and the network must accommodate the newcomer into the schedule somewhere.

It's rare, then, when even the worst or most low-rated show isn't broadcast five or six times before being yanked. But the programs on Channel 6 graced—or disgraced—the airwaves only *once* (or, in the case of *Apple Pie*, twice) before an embarrassed network sent them down the tube.

You're in the Picture
CBS: 1961

You're in the Picture is almost, but not quite, singular in the annals of television history. Although some historians claim that it was yanked from CBS's Friday evening schedule after only a few weeks, this megaflop of a game show instead was canceled after its first airing.

Moreover, the time slot was filled the second week with a program-length apology from the host, who pleaded mea culpa for the feeble-minded attempts at humor and wit incurred the week before.

The host was Jackie Gleason, who was at the time a superbeloved superstar. Gleason was CBS's golden boy with his successes on *The Honeymooners* and *The Jackie Gleason Show*, and the Great One had a long-term contract with the network, guaranteeing him an exorbitant salary for the next fifteen years—even if his services weren't being used at the time. It was CBS's insurance policy against him defecting to a competitor.

Too many years of "To the moon, Alice!" took its toll on the performer, who was famous in the industry for disliking rehearsals. CBS's answer was to create a game show in which the game would be secondary to Jackie's quips and ad-libs. It had worked for Groucho Marx over at NBC for years.

On *You're in the Picture,* a plywood board with painted bodies on it was the major prop, and a guest panel of four celebrities stood behind it, sticking their heads through the holes in the manner of a Coney Island funny-photo booth. The game consisted of them guessing what the picture they formed might be, à la *What's My Line?* It was all, of course, merely a format that would allow Gleason to cut up and crack wise with the contestants and celebrities. Gleason wasn't thrilled with either the game or the opportunity to be the new Bill Cullen, but the CBS bigwigs were adamant. And they were the ones with the checkbooks.

For the first and only show (Friday, January 20, 1961), the panel

How sweet it is. The king of television, Jackie Gleason, surveys his kingdom at Miami Beach following the one-night-only failure of *You're in the Picture.*

consisted of Pat Carroll, Jan Sterling, Arthur Treacher, and Keenan Wynn. The set had a sort of space-age modern look suitable for telecasting—chiaroscuro Jetsons. Gleason himself was nattily turned out in a dark suit with boutonniere.

And that, as it turned out, was the only thing that went right for a whole 30 minutes of prime time. The game itself was convolutedly stupid: Sure, a child could understand it, but he wouldn't want to play it. Neither Gleason nor his panel was funny, and the whole enterprise had the esprit de corps of an afternoon on the chain gang.

"The show was such a disaster that I draw a blank every time I try to explain the format," blasted Jumpin' Jackie Flash. "The only good show was the second one—in which I apologized for the first one."

That's right. After the first telecast, Gleason canceled his own show. CBS swallowed—hard—but accepted the decision.

Viewers who tuned in a week

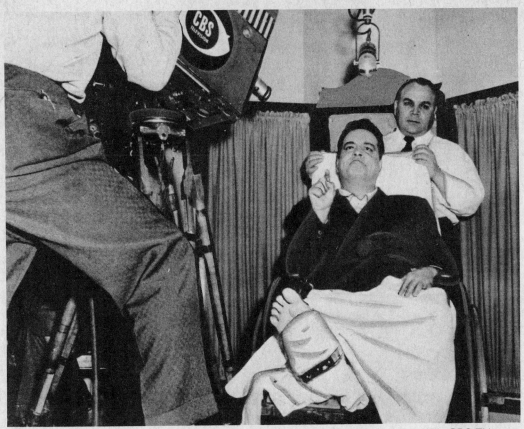

What a Trooper: When he was down with a broken leg, Jackie Gleason broadcast his CBS TV show from his hospital bed. Even the mighty Gleason, however, couldn't pull off a second telecast of his god-awful game show, *You're in the Picture*. How sweet it isn't!

later found Jackie seated in a chair in front of a plain black curtain; *You're in the Picture* was definitely out of the picture. He wore a three-piece suit with a natty carnation, and his only props were his ubiquitous cigarette and drink. What followed was a half-hour comedy monologue masquerad-

ing as an apology for *You're in the Picture,* and the public loved it.

If *You're in the Picture* accomplished anything, it proved that Jackie Gleason was a class act. After all, can anyone imagine Chuck Barris offering a feature-length apology for *3's a Crowd*?

Turn-On

ABC: 1969

"Gimme just one more night," sang British rocker Phil Collins in his Grammy-winning song of the same name. "One more night—with you."

It could have been the song George Schlatter, creator of *Rowan & Martin's Laugh-In*, was singing right after his new "baby," *Turn-On*, was pulled from the ABC lineup after airing *once*. Precisely once, on February 5, 1969. On February 6, ABC executives gathered in a panic to discuss whether it would ever air again. And, in what the *L.A. Times* called "perhaps the fastest action by a network since the days of the quiz scandals," the answer was "no." The yanking made *Turn-On* one of the most expensive one-night stands in history; after all, the usual half-hour encounter, even with dinner and wine beforehand, doesn't run in excess of a million dollars.

Schlatter's reputation for innovation led the Bristol-Myers Corporation, makers of Pepto-Bismol, to come knocking on his door in 1968. The medicine men were looking to sponsor a show that would be highly rated, popular, and would take the country by storm with its uniqueness. In short, they were looking for another *Laugh-In*, which had America spouting "Sock it to me," "You bet your bippy," and "Here come de judge." Bristol-Myers, of course, wanted to sponsor a show that would have America saying "Pepto-Bismol."

"We were told specifically to do something progressive, provocative, adult, controversial, and inventive," remembered Schlatter. He and partner Digby Wolfe cooked up an abbreviated, more outrageous form of *Laugh-In*, and titled the show *Turn-On*. They spent a year developing it into a combination of old-style, nonsensical burlesque comedy mixed with thoroughly modern humor. The result was a show, Schlatter claimed, that was much closer to his original concept of *Laugh-In* than *Rowan & Martin's Laugh-In* turned out to be.

Where *Laugh-In* featured guest stars each week, as well as cameos from personalities as diverse as Ralph Nader and Richard Nixon, *Turn-On*'s main feature was a large computer that frequently flashed on screen, giving the impression of a computer-generated comedy show. A pulsing soundtrack was created out of what was referred to as "electronic music"; Kraftwerk and synthesizers weren't yet part of the music scene. The whole show was stitched together with split-second editing and fast cuts that made *A Hard Day's Night, The Monkees,* and even *Laugh-In* look positively geriatric.

If all these techniques and innovations sound familiar, they should; they became de rigueur in the 1980s when rock videos, MTV, and synthesized sound revolutionized American pop culture. In 1968 and 1969, though, such ultramodern touches weren't foresighted or groundbreaking; they were disturbing. Throwing off the yoke of convention and selling *Turn-On* to an audience accustomed to *The Red Skelton Show* was not going to be easy.

Turn-On was offered to CBS, the top-rated network, and NBC, where *Rowan & Martin's Laugh-In* had found a receptive home. Both turned it down. "It was not any good," said an NBC executive. "It wasn't funny, to begin with. And in many areas it was in bad taste."

CBS's criticism was, in retrospect, particularly telling. "It was so fast with the cuts and chops," said an official, "that some of our people actually got physically disturbed by it!"

ABC, the third-rated network, whose only hits were the gray-bearded *Bewitched* and *The F.B.I.*, could afford to take more chances—especially with a clone of another network's successful show, and especially with George Schlatter and Bristol-Myers behind the project. After ABC executives looked at a reworked pilot, *Turn-On* was tentatively scheduled to take the Wednesday night slot occupied by *Peyton Place.* Schlatter and his producer, Ed Friendly, negotiated a contract that called for creative freedom and an eighteen-episode commitment from ABC.

The premiere date was set for the first week of February 1969, and the production company opted to air neither of the pilots that had been shown to the networks. An episode with veteran comedian Tim Conway was selected instead, obviously in the hope that viewers might be lured into watching by the introduction of one familiar ingredient into an avant-garde casserole.

According to the ratings services, somewhere between 16,000,000 and 17,000,000 people did just that. By and large, they didn't like what they saw. And the Schlatter began to hit the fan.

They saw a string of burlesque-style blackout sketches, à la *Laugh-In,* but far spicier. (A gorgeous woman, about to be shot by a firing squad, is informed that though it may be a bit unorthodox, the *firing squad* has one last request.)

They saw some non sequitur catchphrases dancing across the screen, but none of them were anything like LOOK THAT UP IN YOUR FUNK & WAGNALLS or BEAUTIFUL DOWNTOWN BURBANK. (The one that stuck in everyone's mind—and craw—read: THE AMSTERDAM LEVEE IS A DIKE.)

They saw . . . they saw . . . they didn't quite know what they saw. One surrealistic bit featured the word SEX, its letters throbbing and pulsating, superimposed over two people who enacted a mating ritual pantomime comprised of equal parts Martha Graham and Hugh Hefner.

Even more disturbing than any of this outrageous humor was the way it was presented—backed with unfamiliar, futuristic, threatening music, coming in a barrage of words, sounds, images, and jokes that made Americans wonder what sort of sugar cubes the *Turn-On* staff used in its coffee.

Turn-On viewers did more than turn it off. They began calling local stations. They began to write to the newspapers. They began to write to the network.

In Philadelphia, ABC affiliate WFIL couldn't handle the number of angry calls. The general manager of Cleveland's WEWS sent a telegram to the president of ABC Television, calling the show "just plain dirty"

and sarcastically noting, "If you naughty little boys have to write dirty words on the walls, please don't use *our* walls."

Across America, the reaction to Schlatter and Friendly's concoction was anything but friendly. Stations in Baltimore, Little Rock, and other cities canceled the program the minute the credits stopped rolling. Even NBC couldn't resist kicking another network when it was down—and the kick landed squarely in the *cojones* of the American Broadcasting Company. "The pilot we saw," sniffed an NBC representative, "was an Academy Award winner alongside the thing ABC put on the air."

By the next morning, the American Broadcasting Company found that *Turn-On* had indeed created a national sensation, but it wasn't the pleasant sort of notoriety that provides free publicity and then quietly disappears. It was a groundswell of anger from across the United States, and ABC felt that it had no choice but to cancel the show immediately, although no formal cancellation banns were ever posted. Instead, ABC preferred to say that planning was being done, "determining future programming." (Some say the cancellation came a day after *Turn-On* aired; others claim that it took forty-eight hours.)

Schlatter himself was told nothing about the cancellation. When he found out, his ire matched that of ABC and Bristol-Myers—whose executives must have been downing gallons of pretty pink Pepto-Bismol.

"We had the most exciting 27-minute series on the air," Schlatter insisted. "If . . . this show is too much for the network, then I look forward to a triumphant return of *My Mother the Car.*"

No, George. *Anything* but that.

Apple Pie

ABC: 1978

Rue McClanahan is hilarious on *The Golden Girls*, and Dabney Coleman is hilarious in whatever he does (*9 to 5*, *Mary Hartman, Mary Hartman*, *Buffalo Bill*), but even their comic talents couldn't overcome the dry crust and saccharine sweetness of *Apple Pie*, a 1978 ABC comedy that lasted two telecasts before falling like a lard soufflé.

Meryl Streep herself might have had trouble with the script. The setting was Kansas City. The time was the Depression. And the premise featured McClanahan as a lonely single hairdresser who decides to form a family by advertising in the local newspaper. The result was more like a mock-apple pie: No matter how you slice it, it still tastes like wet Ritz crackers.

McClanahan, as the zany-but-lovable matriarch "Ginger-Nell Hollyhock" (even the names were precious on *Apple Pie*), managed to recruit a family that was as zany, lov-

able, and just goshdarned wacky as she was. Dabney Coleman played "Fast Eddie," a con man who found himself in the role of Dutch uncle to a blind grandfather (Jack Gilford) and two older children whose quirks were more annoying than amusing. Junior attempted to fly when he wasn't reproducing sound effects at the kitchen table, and daughter Anna Marie spent her days tap dancing around the house in an attempt to become the next Shirley Temple.

The setting, the time period, and the family of allegedly adorable eccentrics were all suspiciously, shall we say, *reminiscent* of the venerable George S. Kaufman play, *You Can't Take It with You*. In the case of *Apple Pie*, however, the question wasn't whether you *could* take it with you; it was what person in his right mind would want to.

A half-hour version of the sixty-minute *Pie* pilot was dished up to the public on September 23, 1978, to massive disinterest. ABC, apparently realizing that one bad *Apple Pie* might spoil the whole sitcom barrel, made a quick decision, and the second installment on the following Saturday proved to be the last.

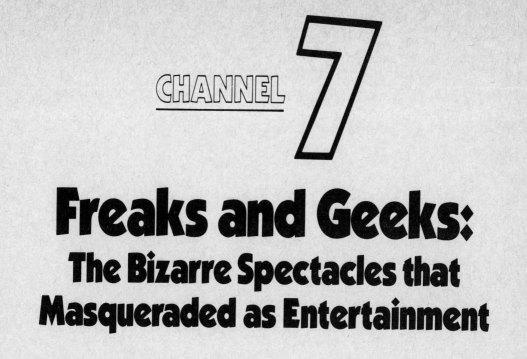

CHANNEL 7

Freaks and Geeks:
The Bizarre Spectacles that Masqueraded as Entertainment

In ancient times, before the dawn of *Leave It to Beaver* and *The Cosby Show*, good wholesome family entertainment often meant an evening at the carnival. Mom, Dad, Junior, and Sis could sit back and watch an assortment of fire-eaters, sword-swallowers, flimflam artists, and lizard-eating geeks, considering it an evening well spent.

This prurient voyeurism is alive and well today televised in activities like pro wrestling. The shows on Channel 7 cater to the darker side of the human spirit—entertainment that is best watched in embarrassed solitude, with the shades drawn and the phone taken off the hook.

That's Incredible!

ABC: 1980–1984

A man runs through a tunnel of fire in a "fire-retardant" suit, emerging with severe burns and what his lawyer refers to as "two charred stumps" where his hands used to be. THAT'S INCREDIBLE!

A stuntman tries to jump over two cars heading toward him at one hundred miles an hour. He bounces painfully off the windshield of car number one, and smashes into the windshield of the second one. His leg twists twice around his knee before he hits the ground.

THAT'S INCREDIBLE!

A young motorcyclist attempts to upstage Evel Knievel by jumping the fountain in front of Las Vegas's Caesar's Palace. He instead hits a concrete wall (at 80 miles per hour). Result: a tear in his aorta as well as fractures in both legs and his pelvis. At the site, one eyewitness claims that fascinated spectators dip their fingers in a pool of the daredevil's blood.

THAT'S INCREDIBLE!

The show that broadcasts such stunts is enormously popular, often ranking just behind *60 Minutes* and *Three's Company* in the ratings.

That's truly incredible—and truly sick.

TV Guide called it a "video version of the *National Enquirer*." *People* said it was a "hybrid of *60 Minutes* and *The Gong Show* designed by a network Dr. Strangelove." It was called, appropriately enough, *That's Incredible!*

No programmer ever went broke underestimating the taste of the viewing public, and *That's Incredible!* was no more than a carnival geek show brought into American living rooms and refined for suburban sensibilities.

While animal rights groups would have raised the henhouse if *That's Incredible!* had shown a man biting off the head of a chicken carnival-style, no one seemed to care when a stuntman tried to catch a .22-caliber bullet between his teeth. (That's inedible!)

"The show needs no justifica-

An Up With People reunion? Nope, just the toothy stars of *That's Incredible!*, the show that managed to injure three stuntmen severely in its quest to thrill jaded suburbanites.

tion," commented *That's Incredible!* producer Alan Landsburg. "We are paying people reasonably well to go out and do incredible stunts for us. . . . An unsuccessful stunt does our program no good. If it's gore, we don't show it." (The biting-the-bullet segment and the tunnel-of-fire routine were aired.)

Ah, but what they did show. Viewers thrilled to the sight of a man suspended by his heels over a pool of sharks, as well as that of a woman covered with bees.

All this merrymaking would have seemed incomparably sleazy if presented by an oily carnival barker, but *That's Incredible!* was instead hosted by three slices of white bread, whose major credentials as journalists were their gleaming, toothy smiles: John Davidson, Cathy Lee Crosby, and Fran Tarkenton.

"I love the show," said Crosby, defending *That's Incredible!* from its detractors. "It offers a better way of entertainment. Fran, John, and I are like the Three Musketeers, encouraging people to develop their potential."

It's unlikely that Crosby, an intelligent woman, included burning one's fingers to stumps in that description. But Tarkenton was even more outrageous and callous in his defense: "We're doing positive, educational things. Teachers are having students watch. People risk their lives every time they get on an airplane. Human triumph means risk; this show celebrates human triumph on all levels."

Davidson was more honest in his assessment. "I laugh at it," he said. "I can't believe it's in the Top 10. A man came up to me and thanked me for a show that was educating his kids rather than some dumb sitcom. Well, if he thinks it's educating his kids, he's kidding himself. . . . It's good exposure, only one day a week and a lot of money."

And money, of course, was what it all boiled down to. The educational value of watching a rooster playing tic-tac-toe or seeing a man lying between two nail-studded slabs of wood could only lead viewers to imitate—spawning the catchphrase "Kids: Don't try this at home!" After all, producer Landsburg and crew didn't want to find themselves on the wrong end of a lawsuit if some dimwitted ten-year-old attempted hopping the family swimming pool on his Schwinn.

That's Incredible!–bashing soon became a favorite sport in the media. *Time* named it "Most Sadistic Show" in its 1980 media awards. *People* printed a damning essay. Garry Trudeau satirized the program in several installments of "Doonesbury." And even *60 Minutes'* Morley Safer got into the fray by proclaiming the so-called "reality shows" like *Incredible!* and *Real People* "the worst brew of bad taste yet concocted by the network witches." *TV Guide*'s 1982 exposé of the behind-the-scenes manipulations of the show's fantastic stunts couldn't even put a crimp in the ratings.

Bad things never last forever, and *That's Incredible!* ruled the roost on ABC's Monday night schedule before succumbing in 1984 to public ennui with arrow-catching daredevils and cigarette-smoking chickens.

During its four-year run, *That's Incredible!* may have achieved a new low in American television—a low likely to be unmatched until some enterprising programmer obtains the right to televised executions. Its appeal was most honestly addressed by a man named George Englund, who produced the filming of the Caesar's Palace motorcycle jump.

"Everybody in this business caters to ratings," he explained. "That's the business. They are reality shows and they go for the ratings. This isn't some deep seminar on American culture."

True. But the fact that *That's Incredible!* consistently topped the Nielsen ratings may say more about American culture than any seminar would be able to reveal.

Hot Seat

SYNDICATED: 1981–

Everyone knows Phil "The Human Animal" Donahue, whose daily talk program deals with everything from thermonuclear war to thermonuclear male strippers. But do you know about *Hot Seat*, starring . . . one . . . Wally George?

Like Phil Donahue, George confronts political and moral issues with the help of guests and a studio audience—and, like Phil, Wally sports an impressive coiffure of silver hair. But that's where the resemblance ends. Consider:

Phil's audience never comes to tapings bearing picket signs with slogans like NUKE THE FAGS.

Phil rarely calls his guests "scum," "slime," or the ever-popular "jerk."

Phil doesn't have security guards stationed on the set who often forcibly eject guests from the program.

And Phil never cites Joe McCarthy and Richard Nixon as his personal heroes.

All this and more happens every week on *Hot Seat*, under the Red-baiting gaze of one of America's most notorious conservative broadcasters, Wally George. The show started as a low-budget public affairs show on tiny KDOC-TV in Anaheim, California, a UHF station owned by fundamentalist Pat Boone. But George's combative interviewing "techniques" took Southern California by storm in the 1980s, and soon *Hot Seat* was syndicated across the nation.

Hot Seat—a purported exchange of ideas that was more like a schoolyard bout of name-calling than anything else—had more to do with pro wrestling than with *Meet the Press*.

A typical *Hot Seat* began with a sweeping pan of the audience—mostly high school and college-age young men decked out in redneck paraphernalia and shouting at the top of their rowdy lungs: *"Wal-lee! Wal-lee!!"* Banners (WALLY FOR PRESIDENT!) and American flags were

On every episode of *Hot Seat*, mercurial host Wally George managed to strike the famous pose of one of his favorite presidents, Richard Nixon. *Gary Leonard*

waved at the camera like the "Hi, Mom" signs at an NFL game.

This was the cue for George, seated behind a cheap plywood desk, to flash his incisors at the crowd and make the "V for Victory" sign. His hair was combed carefully forward into a silver helmet, disguising a large bald spot and skillfully masking his true age (which was variously reported in the media as somewhere between late forties and mid-fifties). Behind the desk hung an American flag and a dime-store portrait of John Wayne, flanked by two beefy security guards.

Hot Seat warmed up with the reading of letters to the show, which generally read one of two ways:

Dear Wally:
You are the only patriotic American on the air today, and I just wanted to tell you to keep giving it to the Commies. God bless America, and God bless you, Wally. . . .

These were the letters that would send the studio audience into bigger paroxysms of demented cheering. The other standard Wally letter read something like this:

Hey Wally!
You and your show both STINK!! I am a liberal (or feminist, or Communist, or homosexual). . . .

These letters were rarely finished: Wally would tear them up and toss the bits in the air while the audience chanted, *"Jerk! Jerk! Jerk!"*

By this point in the show, novice Wally-watchers were beginning to discover that they weren't in Kansas anymore, Toto. If there was any question, though, it was dispelled when George's first guest took the "hot seat" for what the *L.A. Times* called "insult hour."

If the guest was an advocate of abortion George was likely to begin the questioning with "So why are you in favor of killing babies?" If the guest was a feminist, George cited Biblical injunctions "against" feminism. And, God forbid, if the bottom in the hot seat happened to belong to a homosexual, George might ask, "Why aren't you wearing a dress tonight, sweetheart?" as the audience screamed its lungs out, often drowning out any dialogue that might be taking place onstage.

Hot Seat, buried in a Saturday late-night time slot, drew electron-microscopic ratings for its tiny TV station until some of the antics on the show began to turn truly bizarre and downright violent. A stripper called to defend her profession on the show began demonstrating her art on camera before being carried out in the arms of the security guards; the strip came as no surprise, however, as George had obviously manipulated the woman into it. Another guest, a drug advocate who seemed to have been dug up from beyond some Grateful Dead fringe, managed to state his view that "the Bible is the work of the Devil" before George had him thrown off in a paroxysm of fury.

But it was antiwar activist Blase Bonpane who managed to bring the most media attention to *Hot Seat*. He and Wally hit the headlines when they engaged in a screaming match over the propriety of invading Grenada, which culminated in George grabbing Bonpane and shouting, "Get the hell out of my studio!"

Bonpane, an ex-Marine, didn't stay to question George about his use of such un-Christian language; he merely overturned George's desk on his way out the door, which set Wally to new heights of screeching.

George actually screeched his way into the pages of *People* with this little contretemps, which managed to turn his minor Southern California cult into a minor national one. And it was inevitable that Fred Silverman, always Freddie-on-the-spot when there was a buck to be made in the TV biz, would take an interest in the

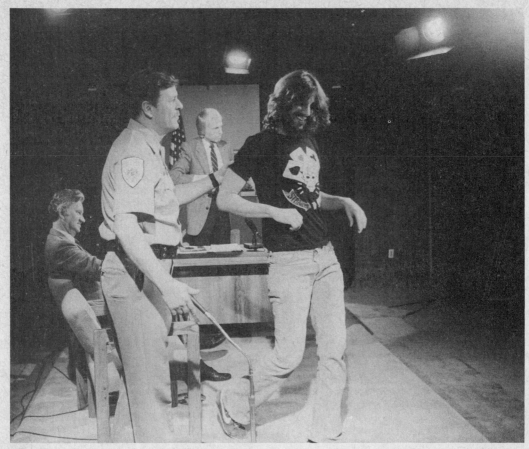

"The Bible is the work of the Devil!" claimed this guest, seconds before Wally George had him ejected from the Hot Seat. *Gary Leonard*

show. Soon Metromedia had a franchise to syndicate *Hot Seat* across the country, and it looked like America might be a Wally World.

That was when the media began digging, and soon it was apparent that Wally's past didn't really jibe with his current position as the great American voice of conservatism.

Although Wally officially claimed to have been married only twice, siring only two children, court records revealed that Mr. God-and-Family had actually been married a total of *five* times—putting him neck and neck with the Gabor sisters in the Nuptial Sweepstakes.

Moreover, his fifth marriage was ended, according to court documents, because "at the time of marriage, defendant said he had only one prior marriage and only two children. In truth and fact, defendant had married four times and had four children, two of whom he admitted he had never seen, did not know their whereabouts and did not contribute to their support."

This dark revelation might have passed as well, if snoopy reporters hadn't ferreted out the identity of one of George's daughters. She turned out to be actress Rebecca De Mornay, the steamy star of the box-office smash *Risky Business*. De Mornay had severed all contact with her father, and her publicist would only say, "She really doesn't want to be used by him to further his career."

And exposure seemed to be what Wally wanted. He soon appeared on his arch-enemy's program, *Donahue*, on which the normally sedate audience booed him; he walked off the show during the last five minutes, guaranteeing more prefab controversy. Soon after that, he brought *Hot Seat* to the radio on several L.A. stations, never managing to stay in one place too long.

Wallymania only lasted in California for a few years (though the show went on), and *Hot Seat* never managed to catch on nationally except as a cult curio.

In 1987, wacky Wally thrust himself back into the headlines when he announced plans to run for mayor of Los Angeles in 1988, attempting to defeat the city's four-term mayor, Tom Bradley. Bradley, pressed for a reaction to the announcement, issued a terse statement that lumped George in with other fringe candidates. Wally, always aware of the value of publicity, didn't mind. He even took a camera crew with him when he went to L.A. City Hall to obtain candidacy papers, literally stopping nonplussed citizens in the halls of City Hall and trying to enlist their support. It made for great footage on the following week's installment of *Hot Seat*.

To the faithful, Wally was the most fun figure they had seen since Tim Curry donned Spandex in *The Rocky Horror Picture Show*, but for most people, *Hot Seat* eventually went the way of all fads. In the final analysis, TV viewers found the five-times-married crusader for the American Way to be the personification of what his audience had chanted for years:

"Jerk! Jerk! Jerk!"

Mr. Television:
The Videodyssey of McLean Stevenson

Ask Mr. or Ms. John Q. Nielsen who they think most rightly deserves the title of Mr. Television, and they're likely to give you the name of some small-screen superstar like Bill Cosby, Milton Berle, Red Skelton, or Ed Sullivan.

There's one man, however, whose TV track record smashes all their records as easily as Hank Aaron sent his 715th home run over the fence. Consider the shows on which "he" was a regular:

The Doris Day Show: 1969–71
The Tim Conway Comedy Hour: 1970

M*A*S*H: 1972–75
The McLean Stevenson Show: 1976–77
Celebrity Challenge of the Sexes: 1978
In the Beginning: 1978
Hello, Larry: 1979–80
Condo: 1983
America: 1985

Obviously, this brave pioneer's accomplishments are too vast to be summed up briefly. That's why Channel 8 is currently broadcasting excerpts from the lifetime output of TV's true demigod. Say *Hello* to *Larry* himself, McLean Stevenson.

Hello, Larry
NBC: 1979–1980

Hello, Larry was anything but a TV start for McLean Stevenson; it was his seventh attempt at small-screen stardom. He had toiled as a regular on *The Doris Day Show* for two years and served as resident buffoon on *The Tim Conway Comedy Hour* before landing the plum role of hapless Henry Blake on *M*A*S*H*. As a member of the 4077th, Stevenson had it all: fame, fortune, and a show that was both highly popular and critically lauded.

Three years of playing second banana to Alan Alda was enough, and Stevenson bade goodbye to *M*A*S*H* without regrets. (Regrets would have been useless anyway; the *M*A*S*H* production team obligingly killed off his character in a plane crash.)

Off he went to NBC and *The McLean Stevenson Show*, a domestic situation comedy that relied mostly on Zany Mix-Ups, Wacky Scrapes, and Madcap Situations in an attempt to wring laughs out of the audience.

Further adding to the purported fun was the presence of that ultimate sitcom annoyance, the Live-in Mother-in-Law. It was whisked off the air within a month, and returned for another few weeks' airing before vanishing forever.

The giant belly flop of *The McLean Stevenson Show* made its star take two steps back on TV's "Chutes and Ladders" game. He next cropped up as the cohost and coach on CBS's *Celebrity Challenge of the Sexes*. That banal contest of gender supremacy lasted precisely five telecasts.

CBS quickly returned McLean Stevenson to the arena where he was believed to be most proficient: situation comedy. The network held high hopes for *In the Beginning*, which it slotted on Wednesday evenings, right after the smash hit *The Jeffersons*.

In the Beginning teamed Stevenson with Priscilla Lopez, the Tony-winning star of *A Chorus Line*, as an uptight, by-the-Good-Book priest

Rosaries are red/McLean was Blue/When CBS canceled/*In the Beginning,* too.

and a streetwise, hip nun. The setting was a Skid Row mission in downtown Baltimore, and the network was hoping for *Hell Town* with laughs. What they got instead was simply hell, and CBS execs were left counting the losses on their rosary beads when *In the Beginning* went from its Genesis to Revelation in less than a month.

A lesser man might have thrown in the sitcom towel after this latest vanquishment in a series of great defeats, but NBC was willing to give McLean Stevenson another whirl. Three months and one week after *In the Beginning* saw its ending, Stevenson once again flip-flopped networks to make his debut in *Hello, Larry.*

Even in the fast-moving TV industry, it was remarkable for any actor to flush a series down the tube in October and manage to be back on another network, with another sitcom ready to air, in only three months. Any show under that strain would have to show a few rough edges, but *Hello, Larry* was all rough edges and no smooth talk.

In this latest guise, Stevenson played a radio talk show host who was greeted with the title phrase by his callers. And in place of character or genuine laughs, NBC and the show's writers layered *Hello, Larry* with some of the most predictable sitcom characters ever to escape from Central Casting: It was as if every single one of TV's worst clichés had taken up residence on one program. Larry had two precocious daughters left over from his marriage (shades of *One Day at a Time*), and Larry was left perpetually unprepared for their developing bodies, lustful boyfriends, and inevitable wisecracks about sex.

At his radio station, Larry worked for—gasp!—a *woman*, and was forced to deal with her as well as the requisite Fat Guy on the staff. As the show continued, Larry's geriatric-but-still-wisecracking father moved in with the family. And in one pathetic, desperate ploy to have someone, *anyone*, tune in, the writers had Meadowlark Lemon join the cast.

Playing himself.

What a basketball star was doing living in suburban Portland, Oregon, was anyone's guess, but the executives at NBC apparently thought they had come up with the format that would turn McLean Stevenson into the new Lucille Ball.

Hello, Larry was spun off from a two-part episode of *Diff'rent Strokes*, the comedy about a white millionaire who adopts two impoverished black children in a fit of white nobility. By introducing *Larry* on *Strokes* and positioning the new program directly behind *Strokes*, NBC hoped to graft some of the Gary Coleman audience onto *Hello, Larry*. The strategy worked briefly, but soon the abysmal quality of *Hello, Larry* was making the lackluster *Diff'rent Strokes* look like *The Mary Tyler Moore Show*.

Ratings dipped disastrously, but

Hapless Larry rehearses for his role as the emcee of a nude beauty pageant in a typically brainless moment from *Hello, Larry. NBC*

NBC was used to low ratings; its biggest hits at the time were the middling *Little House on the Prairie* and *Real People*. Since the network had nothing to lose by giving *Hello, Larry* a shot for a while, the program ran on Friday evenings for eight months in 1979 before it left the air in the summer. During the hiatus, the producers continued to refine their rhinestone-in-the-rough (including adding that noted comedian and raconteur, Meadowlark Lemon), before hurling *Strokes* and *Larry* to the wolves on Wednesday nights, where the program bloc prepared to do battle against the CBS movie and *Charlie's Angels*.

Gary Coleman did what McLean Stevenson couldn't do—he kept *Charlie's Angels* at bay. NBC stubbornly hung in there with *Larry* the lemon before bowing to the inevitable in April 1980 and giving *Hello, Larry* the most merciful of mercy killings. Goodbye, Larry.

The jeering and derision that surrounded *Hello, Larry* for fifteen excruciating months seemed to permanently cripple Stevenson's career. If the show had been another brief, embarrassing interlude like *In the Beginning*, yanked within a month and forgotten within the same amount of time, McLean Stevenson could have gone on to another show fairly quickly. As it was, it took three years before Mr. Television could find another project of suitably disastrous quality.

America

SYNDICATED: 1985

Three years after the failure of *Hello, Larry* and all the rest, McLean Stevenson made a tentative TV comeback in a situation comedy called *Condo*, about a down-and-out family (headed by you-know-who) sharing a condominium with an up-and-coming Hispanic family. *Condo* was a tremendous hit, running 14 years before being sold to syndication for a record sum.

Just kidding. *Condo* was on and off the air within four months, during which his old show *M*A*S*H* went off the air in a blaze of glory and ratings. (Poor McLean couldn't even make a guest appearance; his character's body was still feeding the fishes in the Sea of Japan.)

Two years later, the networks must have decided that the country might *never* be ready for a comedy in which McLean Stevenson played a perpetually exasperated family man. After failing with variations on the same theme at all three networks, your average actor would be relegated to dinner theater in a Howard

Johnson's. But McLean Stevenson, as he had already proved, wasn't your average actor.

In 1985, Paramount Television announced its intention to enter the burgeoning "infotainment" field. ("Infotainment" was the cutesy term used to describe shows that combined information and entertainment, à la *PM Magazine* and *Good Morning America*.)

Paramount's entry was to be a syndicated national show that would be all things to all programmers: a talk show, a news show, a magazine show, and more. The new show would be called *America* (with a "c"), and its hosts would be *Real People*'s Sarah Purcell, *General Hospital*'s Stuart Damon, and . . . McLean Stevenson. Some folks never learn.

Paramount spared no expense or trouble preparing *America* for its debut, sensing that it could be a hit on the scale of another Paramount giant, *Entertainment Tonight*. The company budgeted between $20 and $25 million for *America*'s first year,

The premiere of *America* was not the first time that McLean Stevenson looked foolish on television. Nor would it be the last. *Michael Jacobs Photojournalism*

confident that it would pay off in a long-term investment. And although the show was syndicated, it had the potential audience of a network program; before *America* presented itself to America, more than 100 individual stations had purchased the show. In four major cities—New York, Chicago, Los Angeles, and St. Louis—*America* was purchased by CBS affiliates. It looked like the surest thing that McLean Stevenson had landed since *M*A*S*H*.

America's debut in September 1985 was greeted by overwhelming disinterest by the nation of the title. All of Paramount's preparation had resulted in a show aimed at people who found *USA Today* too lengthy and *The Merv Griffin Show* too intellectually taxing. "Lifestyle" features were lighter-than-air fluff, and the few pathetic attempts at contemporary relevance—including a vapid Jerry Falwell interview conducted by Sarah Purcell—made *Hello, Larry* begin to look good.

Stuart Damon, whose gig on *General Hospital* was still open, abandoned ship almost immediately to

Michael J. Fox, the guest on the first taping of *America*, looks puzzled at the hard-hitting questions of Sarah Purcell. (That's Jimmy Cagney on the video screen behind Fox—not a cameo appearance by Max Headroom.) *Michael Jacobs Photojournalism*

Renaissance man McLean Stevenson took time out between flops to act as guest commentator at an Astrodome pigskin match-up. Unfortunately, his TV ventures after *M*A*S*H* were fumbles.

get back to the more substantive world of soap opera. (Damon's departure was so abrupt that Paramount didn't have a chance to revise its ads; he was trumpeted as a cohost long after he had hotfooted it back to sudsland.)

Despite the fact that the show was shaping up as a major bath, Paramount swore that it would dig in its heels for the long run. But the CBS stations, appalled by the ratings and mortified at the reviews, weren't willing to wait. By December, the CBS affiliates in Los Angeles, New York, Chicago, and St. Louis had all canceled the show themselves. And, like rats deserting the sinking Fluff Boat, stations in Atlanta, Tampa, Cincinnati, Cleveland, San Francisco, and elsewhere promptly tossed *America* into the trash bin.

Faced with more defectors than the Bolshoi Ballet, Paramount threw in the towel and announced the cancellation of *America* in mid-December as a sort of cockeyed Christmas present to the nation. It was to have its final airing during the first week of January.

But the final indignity didn't belong to Paramount; it fell squarely on the shoulders of TV's favorite whipping boy. Within days of *America*'s cancellation, Paramount canceled McLean Stevenson. No two weeks' notice—after all, the show was only going to last another two weeks. For the remainder of its run, Purcell was allowed to run the ship on her own.

That was the last of McLean Stevenson's TV work to date.

Although he's racked up enough telembarrassments to qualify as the Bob Uecker of the TV game, a canny boob tube observer would do well not to discount McLean Stevenson just yet. In a few years, some brave programming executive will no doubt be looking for a perpetually exasperated father character for some domestic sitcom, and Stevenson's phone will ring. And the fact that McLean Stevenson has flopped so often with such consistently awful shows says less about him than it does about the myopic sheep of the television industry who have, time and time again, let him run unhousebroken over the airwaves.

Shooting Stars:
The Biggest Telembarrassments of the Biggest Stars

It's risky business when a major star embarks on a new televised endeavor. For every Jane Wyman or Joan Collins making a spectacular transition or comeback on the home screen, there's always a sad case like Mary Tyler Moore, whose variety hour was hooted off the tube, or Elliott Gould, who flopped back-to-back with the sitcoms *E/R* and *Together We Stand*.

But Moore's and Gould's programs were just minor embarrassments compared to the TV travesties now showing on Channel 9. How could the likes of Lana Turner and Lucille Ball meet with such complete and utter disaster?

Meeting of Minds

PBS: 1976–1981

Public television is no more immune to TV travesty than are the commercial networks.

For five years, PBS straddled a fine line between thought-provoking entertainment and classical kitsch with *Meeting of Minds*, a chat show featuring historical figures from various eras gathering for a roundtable discussion. It's hard to believe that this pompous version of *The Merv Griffin Show* actually gathered several prestigious awards during its run.

The program was presided over by the tuxedoed Steve Allen, who created the show and wrote the episodes as well as moderating them. Where Merv might be oohing and aahing over Eva Gabor, Mariette Hartley, and Jack Jones, Steve was more often found in the company of Voltaire, Florence Nightingale, Martin Luther, and Plato. Talk about your tough bookings; even Dick Cavett couldn't get Plato.

The thought of actors in bad makeup portraying historical figures in a talk show format was too much for CBS, ABC, and NBC. All three commercial networks turned it down flat, although a variant on the formula did crop up on *Saturday Night Live* when Dan Aykroyd, playing the pompous Leonard Pinth-Garnell, hosted "Bad Playhouse."

Culture Club: Longtime comedian Steve Allen created and hosted *Meeting of Minds*, a self-important talk show with the likes of Voltaire and Marie Antoinette as guests. *KCET-TV*

Proud hubby Steve Allen looks on as Jayne Meadows emotes her way through her part as Florence Nightingale on *Meeting of Minds.* The makeup job is typically tacky. *KCET-TV*

Steve Allen's pronunciamentos on the show even sounded like Pinth-Garnell. "I find no subject matter more stimulating than philosophy and history," Allen explained. "But my mind does not simply receive impressions. It talks back to the authors, even the wisest of them—a response I'm sure they would warmly welcome."

The first installment of the show featured Thomas Paine, Teddy Roo-

On this edition of *Meeting of Minds,* the guests were the Dowager Empress of China, Tz'u-hsi (Beulah Quo), with her servant; Cesare Beccaria (Robert Carricart); the Marquis de Sade (Stefan Gierash); and Frederick Douglass (Roscoe Lee Browne). Note the fright wig on Browne, and the bowl of fruit on the table in front of Steve Allen. Kulture with a Kapital K. *KCET-TV*

sevelt, Thomas Aquinas, Cleopatra, and Steve Allen, all sitting around a large table, riposting hilariously stuffy dialogue. Surely if any of these real historical people really had any words of wisdom for Steve Allen, the words would have been of the four-letter variety.

None of this mattered to Allen, who saw his show as the intellectual savior of America. "I have a philosophical concern that the American public is getting dumber," he stooped to explain to an interviewer. "So I've done three things. One is *Meeting of Minds.*" (The other two were a record album entitled "How to Think" and an educational game called "Strange Bedfellows.")

Meeting of Minds' major achievement may have been its addition of one more imponderable question to the TV lexicon. While past generations might have asked "What did Ozzie Nelson *do* for a living?" or "Why did the castaways on *Gilligan's Island* take along complete wardrobes for 'a three-hour tour'?", *Meeting* supplied its own Zen koan:

Why did every major female figure in history bear such a startling resemblance to Jayne Meadows?

Ah, yes. Be it Cleopatra, Madame Curie, or Clara Barton, the woman under the unconvincing (albeit thick) makeup job was always Jayne Meadows, the fiery-haired actress whose greatest fame had come from years of panel duty on some of TV's most enduring game shows, as well as appearances on several of Steve Allen's many weekly programs since the late 1950s.

Ah, yes; Meadows had another illustrious credit. She was married to Steve Allen.

"Jayne has played nearly all the female roles on the show, and her performances have been brilliant," Steve Allen said, adding, "Being married to Jayne is like being married to a dozen brilliant women." If that was true, Meadows might well have starred in a remake of *The Three Faces of Eve*
rather than *Meeting of Minds*, since her performances on the show—as Susan B. Anthony or Elizabeth Barrett Browning or whomever—certainly weren't denying Meryl Streep any sleep. (Jayne Meadows didn't exactly go on to win the lead roles in *Sophie's Choice* or *Sweet Dreams*. Her greatest role after *Meeting of Minds* was as a spokesperson for Mocha Mix, a popular nondairy creamer product.)

Meeting of Minds continues to live on in syndicated PBS reruns, gloriously uninterrupted by Steve and Jayne's homespun Mocha Mix commercials. Fans of "Bad Playhouse" remember the show fondly; after all, it bore the same relationship to intellectual discourse that Liberace's piano technique did to Paderewski's.

Harold Robbins' "The Survivors"

ABC: 1969–1970

One of the most expensive and lavish series ever produced on television was also one of the briefest. During its short run in the last days of 1969, it was involved in more heartbreak and intrigue than its own troubled characters. And the stats are still staggering: Although *Harold Robbins' "The Survivors"* lasted a scant fifteen weeks, it took three producers, two years of planning and almost a year of shooting before one episode was committed to celluloid.

"One of the most expensive flops in television history," says *Variety*. "One of the stormiest, most publicized series in TV history," concurs the book *The Films of Lana Turner*. And Turner herself remembers the show's cancellation banns with characteristic understatement: "As an actress, I can't say I was stunned when I got the news."

Its rather pompous title was *Harold Robbins' "The Survivors,"* by contractual agreement with the soap's creator. (According to Turner, the flash-trash writer had made a cool million dollars for a one-page, triple-spaced outline of the show.) And although other writers never felt the compulsion to title the screen versions of their books with monickers like *Harper Lee's "To Kill a Mockingbird"* or *Alice Walker's "The Color Purple,"* ABC must have thought that the Robbins name would help boost the ratings on its own merits—or demerits.

The network held such high hopes for the show, in fact, that they lured a silver screen star to play the lead. That dubious honor went to Lana Turner, whose sexpot image had waned a bit during the 1960s, but whose ability to jerk a tear or two was still apparent in pictures like *Madame X* and, of course, *Peyton Place*.

Hollywood makes strange bedfellows, and Robbins and Turner were two of the strangest, considering her well-known antipathy for the writer.

It was April 1958 when Turner and her lover, Johnny Stompanato, were having one of their regular screaming matches, but it was cut short—literally—when the star's teenage daughter Cheryl Crane came into the room and stabbed her mother's boyfriend to death. The sensational nature of the crime, which resulted in a verdict of justifiable homicide in the ensuing court case, kept Turner in the public eye for months.

Robbins soon came out with a novel bearing more than a slight resemblance to the Crane-Stompanato case, titling his book *Where Love Has Gone.* It was made into a hit film in 1964, and the movie managed to keep the grisly case discussed in the media long after it would have been relegated to the pages of *Hollywood Babylon.*

"I hated the man," said Turner in her autobiography *Lana: The Lady, The Legend, The Truth.*

So why did she do the show?

Turner's autobiography doesn't make that quite as clear as her feelings toward Robbins, but her ex-husband Robert Eaton remembers, "I introduced Lana to Robbins. She disliked him at first, but as soon as the almighty dollar was visible they became friends."

Dollars aplenty would be visible throughout the production of *The Survivors*, as it was to be one of the most expensive series attempted to date. Turner's character, Tracy Carlyle Hastings, was also a fairly juicy dame.

Although Turner's character was of glamorous middle age (like Linda Evans and Joan Collins in *Dynasty*), she had a whale of a past, a hell of a present, and an uncertain future. Her son Jeffrey, played by "new discovery" Jan-Michael Vincent, had been conceived during a tryst with old flame Antaeus (Rossano Brazzi)—a fact that her current husband Philip (Kevin McCarthy) could hardly object to, since he spent much of his time hopping from boudoir to boudoir himself. In fact, McCarthy, whose most famous role was the lead in the science fiction classic *Invasion of the Body Snatchers,* spent much of *The Survivors* snatching bodies—and vice versa.

Turner and company signed contracts for twenty-six hour-length episodes of the show, indicating ABC's commitment to making *The Survivors* a real survivor in the ratings game. Although the pieces were all there, they just never seemed to get assembled. As Turner recalled: "Many months went by but not a single script was written about the jet-set family of a banking tycoon. Writers were hired and fired every day, it seemed. . . . Before anyone ever developed a single show, we set off for the Riviera to shoot background scenes for the stories that would somehow evolve."

Hmm. According to other sources, it was La Turner herself who kept the production team reaching for Anacin, Maalox, and Valium. It began with a brief item in *Variety:*

In the first week of shooting her first vid-pic series, Lana Turner was involved in a physical and verbal hassle with her producer, and he is no longer with the series.

An argument on the set had turned into a slapping match between Turner and producer William Frye, and it was bye-bye, Frye.

Later, costume designer Luis Estevez took a powder when an article quoted Turner as saying that her wardrobe was a bit matronly. "They have to make my costumes each weekend because until Friday night they don't know what they'll be doing Monday," she caviled.

Hell hath no fury like a costumer scorned, and Estevez comported himself with biting wit. "I've been super-kind to Lana for over a year," he said. "I deserve the Croix de Guerre for that. . . . Perhaps it was not my designs that made her look matronly. After all, nothing is forever."

More strife came from the fact that Turner, despite her long career, wasn't the top-billed star of the show. That honor went to Mr. Tan-Man himself, George Hamilton, who played Turner's swinging brother Duncan. (Hamilton also received $17,500 a week, while Turner had to scrape by on $12,000.)

To add personal injury to professional insult, Turner's sixth marriage went to pieces while *The Survivors* was filming on location. She and husband Robert Eaton divorced when they returned from the Riviera, and Lana married husband number seven, Ronald Dante.

All this stress began to reach ridiculous heights when the pampered Turner clashed head-on with the bare-bones exigencies of the weekly TV grind. Her habit of taking a wheelchair from curb to plane through public airports was known within the Hollywood community, but when she expected similar treatment on the set of the already beleaguered *Survivors*, fireworks flew. Turner demanded use of a limousine, not only from her home to the set, but around the lot itself.

"I want to know that car is there outside the stage at every moment," Turner said. "I said I might just have to go to the ladies' room, and I won't use the one on the stage. I only go to my permanent dressing room. It's a block away, and I won't walk. Not that I *can't*, but just because I have gone into another medium doesn't mean that I'm going to change my way of living and working."

If ABC was spending all its time pampering Turner's gold-plated bowels, how could it hold in the reins on its gold-plated soap opera? All the footage, except for the background shots, that had been filmed in Europe had to be discarded as the scripts changed, wasting millions of dollars.

The network could only hold its breath (and its nose) as it unleashed

Harold Robbins' "The Survivors" was a multi-million-dollar debacle that lasted for three months in 1969. Its stars were Kevin McCarthy, Lana Turner, and the eternally tanned George Hamilton.

Harold Robbins' "The Survivors" on Monday nights, where its competition was *Mayberry R.F.D.* and the NBC Monday Night Movie. *The Survivors*, however, had gone through so much *tsuris* that the network only shot fifteen episodes instead of the originally planned twenty-six. If *The Survivors* didn't manage to do what its title implied, ABC stood to save millions of dollars.

Sure enough, the Andy Griffithless *Mayberry* handily clobbered the histrionics on ABC, and *Harold Robbins' "The Survivors"* was dead meat. The remaining eleven episodes were never shot, and the program that began with such promise in September of 1969 was gone by the end of the following January.

Turner's contract was settled by paying her for half the remaining episodes, and the network saved a bit more money by rerunning the show during the following summer, instead of spending the cash to develop a limited-run summer show. Thrifty ABC even cut several of the episodes together to make made-for-TV movies.

In 1982, Turner returned to the world of nighttime soaps, costarring opposite Jane Wyman on *Falcon Crest*. In her one-season appearance, it is not known whether CBS provided limousine service for the grande dame's potty trips.

Aloha Paradise

ABC: 1981

Aloha. It means hello, and good-bye. And in the case of *Aloha Paradise*, it meant both—almost at the same time. Rip-offs are nothing new in TV, but ABC actually ripped itself off with this one, which was a direct cross between *The Love Boat* and *Fantasy Island*. The ABC executives spent big bucks on this chance to eat their own young, but *Aloha Paradise* didn't manage to produce a carbon copy of the other shows' Nielsens; instead, it ended up delivering a Hawaiian punch to the ABC schedule.

Like that long-running syphilis scow *The Love Boat*, *Paradise* featured three revolving stories about people working out their trivial melodramatic problems while on vacation. Like *Fantasy Island*, *Paradise* was populated by a guest-star cast comprised of contemporary TV actors and old warhorses from the golden age of the silver screen. And, like both shows, *Aloha Paradise* gave them a glamorous tropical setting in which to unfold their petty dramas.

Aaron Spelling and Douglas Cramer, the men who oversaw the creation of both *Boat* and *Island*, apparently decided that they could add still more water to the concept and continue to call it milk. Their first move (after settling on Hawaii as a locale) was to hire a big name of yesteryear to be the Gavin MacLeod/ Ricardo Montalban of Oahu. Their choice: Debbie Reynolds.

The pert star of *Singin' in the Rain* had had only one foray into weekly TV before, an ill-fated 1969 sitcom bearing her name that got clobbered by its competition, *The Mod Squad*. Within the industry, *The Debbie Reynolds Show* was still remembered as a troubled program, and Reynolds herself had little affection for it. "I watched *Mod Squad*," she said bluntly.

She was similarly realistic about her new show. "I think when the critics write about this show the major criticism is going to be its similarity to *Love Boat*. How many more paradises can you have? . . . I think it has a similar format in only one area, that we have guest stars and it's episodic."

What Deb forgot to mention was the supporting cast, which had everything except a nasal man shouting "De plane! De plane!" Most visible was Bill Daily, who as Reynolds' sidekick delivered a double dose of the Nervous Norvus routine that he had honed to predictable perfection on *I Dream of Jeannie* and *The Bob Newhart Show*. There was also a cute blonde social director who was a virtual copy of the one aboard *The Love Boat*; in fact, they were so similar that *Aloha*'s social director jumped ship to replace the one on *Love Boat* when she left the show. Debbie's paradise also contained one toothy blonde hunk of a lifeguard, and a Samoan bartender who looked as if she had spent the last twenty years playing Bloody Mary in a road tour of *South Pacific*.

It seemed certain that the audience that followed each cruise of *The Love Boat* with slack jaws would certainly go for *Aloha*, and the producers spared no expense in flying a large production crew to the fiftieth state for a lavish two-hour pilot. In accordance with native custom (and because it was a great publicity angle), everyone conducted a native "peace ceremony" in order to appease the gods before filming began. But all the bananas and breadfruit in the world, as they knew, couldn't guarantee ratings success.

Back in the more prosaic environs of a Universal Studios soundstage, a meticulous replica of the Hawaiian hotel was built to match up with the location shots. The crew even ventured over to the CBS lot to shoot some scenes on a mock-tropical lagoon that was left over from the days of *Gilligan's Island*.

The first episode, in February 1981, was launched with the appropriate pomp and flackery befitting a show that, it was believed, would become a long-running and enormously profitable part of the American TV lexicon. When Steve Lawrence, on the soundtrack, broke into the first bars of the schmaltzoid theme song, it was actually a surprise when the words weren't "Love . . . exciting and new. . . ."

Within *Aloha Paradise*'s initial two hours, a dizzying array of has-beens (Van Johnson, Louis Jourdan, Dana Wynter, Lorne Greene, and the indefatigable Jayne Meadows) and never-will-bes paraded by in the usual stock situations, buoyed by the Mary Worth helpfulness of Reynolds and bolstered by the wicky-wacky antics of her staff. (In future weeks, *Aloha Paradise* seemed to pluck its "stars" straight off game-show panels, with guests like Lisa Hartman, Randolph Mantooth, and Bert Convy.)

Critics, predictably, moaned. The *L.A. Times* said that *The Love Boat* was "a veritable *Citizen Kane* compared to this piece of nonsense . . . everything but the kitchen sink—which is probably guest starring next week. This is Paradise???"

None of this would matter, of course, if the public clutched Debbie and friends to their hearts. But when the ratings came in, it seemed that the island gods weren't happy with the offerings left behind by the crew. (Perhaps they wanted a virgin, and we all know how hard *they* are to find in Hollywood.) Viewership dropped precipitously in following weeks, and the Spelling-Cramer company was sadly forced to conclude that, in this case, *Aloha* really meant goodbye.

The show was too expensive to keep producing if no one was going to watch, and the public definitely preferred *The Love Boat* to Debbie Does Honolulu.

Within a few months, *Aloha Paradise* had bitten the dust, and it was a wrap for Reynolds. "Carrie Fisher's mother" was then free to pursue a nightclub act with Donald O'Connor, as well as produce *Do It Debbie's Way*, a best-selling aerobics videotape that featured the likes of Rose Marie and Shelley Winters huffing and puffing their way to svelteness. For Aaron Spelling and the countless "stars" who counted on shows like *Aloha* for their daily bread, it was truly a loss. Maybe, if they'd had Charo on the first episode . . .

Saturday Night Live with Howard Cosell

ABC: 1975–1976

"Live—from New York!!" came this show, but it wasn't NBC's groundbreaking late-night comedy show with Chevy Chase, Gilda Radner, et al. ABC's *Saturday Night Live with Howard Cosell* bore about as much resemblance to that brilliant show as *Terms of Endearment* did to the pornographic rip-off *Sperms of Endearment*.

ABC's attempt to revive the old variety show format wasn't a dumb idea—at least, no dumber than most TV decisions. All the network needed was a variety of fresh faces with a smattering of talent in various fields of expertise, and a moderately funny, charismatic host who was willing to play second banana to the acts on his show. Most important, the host had to be someone that America already knew and loved.

For this sensitive role, ABC picked . . . Howard Cosell.

The laughs pealed through the television industry long and loud. Marvin Antonowsky, vice-president of programming at competing NBC, expressed his confidence that the show would last a total of four weeks. But what were the slings and arrows of a jealous industry compared to the talent, erudition, and sheer windbaggery of the Mighty Mouth of *Monday Night Football*?

Cosell had been fed up with the puerile world of pro football for a while—referring to the sport as "the toy department of life." His thespian career, meanwhile, had always been visible under his sportscaster facade, honed with guest shots on shows like *The Odd Couple, The Partridge Family*, and the immortal *Nanny and the Professor*.

SNL with Howard C. was dreamed up by Cosell himself, with the help of his longtime executive producer Roone Arledge. (No one questioned the wisdom of having a football commentator and the head of ABC Sports collaborating on a variety program.) The two concocted a plan for a live television show, with segments beamed in from around the world on satellite; Humble Howard

The ever modest sportscaster, Howard Cosell, proved himself no Ed Sullivan when he hosted a short-lived variety hour now known as "the other *Saturday Night Live*."

would be the thread that tied all the elements together.

"Roone and I don't want to make horses' asses out of ourselves," Cosell assured the public. And the Toupeed One didn't waste an opportunity to build the show—and himself—up with his own peculiar brand of florid prose. A few samples:

"I'm not going to do what I don't do well. I am not going to sit on a horse, pretending to be Cher, as I did on the Sonny Bono show."

Or:

"I'm no song-and-dance man. Nor am I a stand-up comic. . . . What I am is a performer with an ability to communicate. I have established credibility in every corner of this country. I have felt the pulse of America. I know who has something to say, what to ask, and when to ask it. Because of this, I will create an intimacy between my guests and the viewing audience.

"We believe *Saturday Night Live* [with Howard Cosell] will become the biggest hit of 1975."

Since the new show was the first in years to be done entirely live, critics could only guess what the results might be; the insouciant Howard, secure in his position as Sullivan reincarnate, was happy to let them speculate. ("Writers are germs who stick together.")

To ensure wide viewership for the inaugural installment, Cosell and Arledge planned an ambitious mélange of genuine talent and star-spangled kitsch. Apparently Arledge and wiser heads at ABC hadn't trusted Cosell to go at it without a powerful backup. In a short demonstration film for potential advertisers, Cosell opined, "You know what's going to make this show? Me. The born superstar. They didn't give me looks, but they gave me an absolute monopoly on brains and talent."

Still, God had apparently sprinkled a bit of the leftover talent elsewhere in the universe, and Arledge and his minions tried to get as much of it as they could for the first show—beginning with the cast of the then-hot Broadway musical *The Wiz*, who performed "Ease on Down the Road" while doing just that through the streets of Manhattan.

Among other talents on the premier were the Bay City Rollers—the hottest "discoveries" of 1975, considered by a gullible few to be the pretenders to the Beatles' throne. (By 1976, though, they were languishing in the Old Fads Home.) Cosell had high hopes for the Rollers' segment, which was to originate "live via satellite" from England. "It is my hope that John Lennon will be onstage to talk to them," Cosell stated before the telecast. "John's a friend of mine, but his wife's pregnant and he's gone into seclusion."

Other "top" acts that were "live via satellite" included Vegas-based animal trainers Siegfried and Roy, Shirley Bassey ("Goooooold-finger!") and Country Boy John Denver, introduced in deathless Cosell hyperbole as "that poet of the mountains." Robert Frost must have slept well that night.

But it was the true oddities that made the first Cosell show look like it was broadcast from a parallel universe. Paul "Havin' My Baby" Anka, debuted the song stylings of a brand-new protégé on the show. Was it a talented unknown from Juilliard? Nope—it was tennis pro Jimmy Connors, who belted out a tune like he was lobbing a fast one across the net. The performance must have sent the talent agents in the audience scrambling to re-sign Shirley Bassey.

Then there were the "live on tape" congratulations from the likes of Senator Lowell Weicker and Senator Ted Kennedy, who had had experience and sympathy for another man who might find himself in deep water. And as a final flourish, Frank Sinatra took the stage with Cosell for one of those duels of insults that pass for entertainment at Hollywood roasts and on inner-city street corners.

Ratings for the first show suggested that the public still found Cosell as abrasive as a Brillo pad—and TV critics' comments confirmed the notion that they weren't crazy about him either.

Week two. Week three. Week four. They all passed in a blur, but there was something bizarre in each telecast, something like an embryonic *Late Night with David Letterman*

played straight. On one memorable show Cosell, apparently buoyed by Jimmy Connors' attempt at song, decided to test his pipes as well—and he picked Barbara Walters to be his Jeanette MacDonald. The two were coached by Andy Williams.

John Wayne dropped by to offer his opinion, Andy Rooney–style, on what should be done with people who make assassination attempts. (The recent attempts on President Ford's life by Squeaky Fromme and Sara Jane Moore suggested that this form of recreation might replace streaking.)

Cosell diplomatically avoided the fact that the Duke never served in the military service that he espoused. The host only listened as Wayne suggested that we "bloody them up a bit," put them before news cameras, and say, "They missed. Think what we would have done to them if they hadn't."

Howard's old friend Muhammad Ali even did a "live via satellite" segment from Manila on the eve of his championship fight with Joe Frazier. Charo did the show; after all, no variety show worth its salt didn't have the coochie-coochie gal on at least once. (Howard, well-known for his prodigious vocabulary, called Charo an "electrifying, vivacious bombshell.")

Even with an electrifying, vivacious bombshell like Charo on board, Cosell never looked comfortable doing the show. Neither had Ed

Sullivan, even after 23 years on the air, but Cosell's show folded before even 23 episodes. Meanwhile, on another network, another program called *Saturday Night Live* was beginning to take the United States by storm.

Cosell, of course, got his career back on track soon afterward, leaving *Monday Night Football* for good and writing a macho-bitchy tell-all book about sportscasting, *I Never Played the Game*. Years later, the man is still remembered for his pompous color commentary, his cigar, his toupee, his heavy-lidded features, his polysyllabic put-downs, his often-imitated vocal delivery.

Remembered, that is, for everything except *Saturday Night Live with Howard Cosell*. In January 1976 that achievement was laid to rest on the scrap heap of pop culture.

Right next to the Bay City Rollers.

Life with Lucy

ABC: 1986

Lucille Ball's television output has been staggering: 179 *I Love Lucy* episodes, 156 *The Lucy Show* episodes, and 144 *Here's Lucy* episodes.

Oh, and a few episodes of something called *Life with Lucy*, a telembarrassment of the highest order that lasted a brief month or so in the mid-eighties. It had been touted as the 75-year-old comedienne's "comeback to television"—a medium Ball had avoided since the dawn of what she called "cheap laughs" and "shock value stuff" of the seventies. After all, it's hard to imagine Lucy Ricardo getting laughs with menopause humor, or Ricky calling Fred Mertz a "Polack."

But the 1980s brought a return to the family-oriented sitcom, and it was the success of *The Cosby Show* and *The Golden Girls* that convinced Lucille Ball that it was time for her brand of comedy again—only not on her old network, CBS.

ABC, the network firmly lodged in third place, was only too willing to take a chance on Lucille Ball. But how can you ask the Queen of Television to do a pilot? You can't, of course, and ABC didn't, crossing its fingers and giving the septuagenarian star carte blanche. The network shoulda got a pilot; as it turned out, one might have suspected that Ball was still working for CBS as a double agent.

The flimsy story that they ended up with cast Ball as Lucy Barker, a little old lady from Pasadena, living with her daughter, son-in-law, and grandchildren. Another member of the household was her late husband's partner, Curtis MacGibbon, a stuffy type who co-owned a hardware store with Lucy. MacGibbon was played by longtime Lucy costar Gale Gordon, who came out of semiretirement at the age of 80 to rejoin his old friend.

No matter how talented the twosome might be, with a cumulative total of 155 years of experience, visions of bones snapping and hips breaking kept everyone worried. After all, Lucy was famous for her physical stunts at an age when many other people were content to play golf or do needlepoint. Could they carry it off?

Yes—and no. Although Ball wasn't expected to roller-skate or parachute onto the set, the character of Lucy Barker *was* conceived as a physical fitness nut, which would give the star myriad opportunities to jog and perform calisthenics—to the exasperation of Gordon and the supposed delight of the studio audience.

It just didn't jell; in fact, it coagulated. The first bad sign came when the network decided not to provide preview episodes to TV critics, preferring instead to let the public make its own decisions. The press ban went as far as the *tapings* themselves; no members of the fourth estate were allowed to watch the show as it was taped. (This technique is often used in Hollywood when a studio has a critical bomb-a-saurus on its hands, like any Sylvester Stallone film without the word *Rocky* in its title.)

When the show finally aired, the public learned why ABC was so chary. *Life with Lucy* was beyond run-of-the-mill bad—it was painful to watch, especially since Lucille Ball, in her heyday, had been so delightful. Viewers, slightly curious the first week, defected in droves forever after, preferring to remember the vital, funny redhead who was married to a Cuban bandleader.

Part of the problem was that Ball and Gordon had no supporting characters worthy of Fred and Ethel. Their family had all the appeal of marshmallow fluff, long on toothy grins and short on everything else; they made the Brady Bunch look as complex and quirky as Hannah and Her Sisters.

And then there were the plots. In the first episode, one of the major laugh-inducing developments consisted of Lucy rearranging the contents of the hardware store into alphabetical order. Even the most devout Lucy fan could only manage a feeble chuckle at this, and no one at all was laughing when Lucy accidentally sold her grandson's teddy bear (and went to small claims court to retrieve it).

By the end of the first month, even a guest appearance by John Ritter couldn't help the ratings. The public had overwhelmingly rejected Lucy, and the critics couldn't even summon the strength to criticize the redheaded American institution. ABC pulled the show from its schedule without fanfare, making it the first casualty of the 1986–87 season.

Fans preferred to forgive and forget, and returned to the syndicated reruns of *I Love Lucy*, still going strong after thirty-five years. As Lucy Ricardo herself might have cried: "Waaaah, *Ricky!*"

The Spice of Life:
Variety Shows that Were the Kiss of Death

Variety may be the spice of life, but the variety shows on Channel 10 are more like the kiss of death. A mixture of songs, jokes, comedy skits, and guest stars can effervesce under the stewardship of Carol Burnett or the original *Saturday Night Live* cast, but it can just as easily curdle in the wrong hands.

If Channel 10 was to broadcast all the merely bad variety hours that TV has shown over the years, there wouldn't be enough hours in the day to catch the likes of *The Captain and Tennille*, *The Brady Bunch Hour*, *Mary*, *The Liberace Show*, *The Tim Conway Show*, and the other vapid and vulgar varieties that have clogged the airwaves over the years. But the all-singing, all-dancing, all-banal shows on Channel 10 are among the most completely bizarre of all time.

Pink Lady and Jeff

NBC: 1980

Mie Nemoto and Kei Masuda were two perfectly nice women who made a laughingstock of the National Broadcasting Corporation in 1980. Their Friday night comedy–variety hour, engineered by mad programmer Fred Silverman and up-and-coming NBC executive Brandon Tartikoff, was designed to be the network's own clone of *Donny and Marie*, but a few small details got in the way—grasp of the English language, for one.

The women were known collectively as Pink Lady and, in the 1970s, Pink Lady's Japanese TV program was the Oriental answer to the Bee Gees or Blondie. In that pre-Madonna age, the women weren't required to writhe on the floor simulating orgasm, but had only to stand on stage, placidly lip-synching their latest bubble gum tunes while the money just rolled in.

Any time money was rolling in, programming czar Fred Silverman was sure to be nearby. Having controlled the fate of both CBS and ABC (and having brought both networks to the top, one after another), Silverman then moved to NBC, where he planned to do exactly the same thing. *Pink Lady* was to be an important rung in that ladder.

Perhaps it was his extensive experience in Saturday morning children's programming that made him see such potential in Pink Lady; after all, the women were as bland as Smurfs and sweet as Strawberry Shortcake.

Pink Lady also came along at just the right time for variety shows. *Donny and Marie* caught ABC's competitors by surprise when it became a major Friday night hit. Since the safest pitches in television are plots that rip off other successful shows, the networks soon had their Eyes out and their Peacock feathers up for an equally successful show featuring a cute, asexual, clean-scrubbed duo.

When the Osmonds were canceled in 1979, Friday night was left with a proven variety-show audience, and no one to satisfy that need. One thing was for sure: NBC was spinning its wheels on Friday night with its lineup of *Shirley* (Jones, that is), the venerable *Rockford Files*, and a cop show with the unpronounceable title *Eischied*.

All these developments conspired to trip up Silverman when Mie and Kei's prodigious ability to sell records happened to catch his attention. Never one to *cherchez* a *femme* when he saw money, Fred signed them to a network contract and set about developing a show that would swell their popularity in America. Like the Monkees, Pink Lady would be a media-created group (in America, at least), and if all went well, they'd be on the side of every fourth-grader's lunchbox within a year.

Actually, the truly big American singing sensations of 1979 were the Village People, a group of men from Greenwich Village who belted out sexually suggestive songs like "In the Navy" and "Y.M.C.A." Clad in leather, body paint, and chaps, they might have been a popular teen draw, but were hardly likely to lure advertisers to the network. Compared to the sexually suspicious Villagers, Mie and Kei looked like Patti Page and Maria von Trapp.

Fred Silverman was nuts about the women; they were cute, produced lucrative records, and could hardly threaten the Bible Belt. He even had a Pink Lady poster on the wall of his office as if his office were a thirteen-year-old's bedroom. A network joke held that the glossy poster had been the pilot for the show that was to become *Pink Lady*.

To help "develop" the show—we've got these women, now what do we do with them?—Silverman enlisted the aid of one Brandon Tartikoff, a bright young light in the industry. Silverman had guided the career of Tartikoff, who was then West Coast vice-president of NBC programs. As 1980 rolled around, Tartikoff was named president of NBC Entertainment (by Silverman), and it was there he enjoyed great success. First, though, came a trial by fire for Brandon-san.

Upon his promotion, Tartikoff was saddled with developing *Pink Lady*, turning Mie and Kei into Donny and Marie. Not an easy task. Some of the differences between Mie and Kei and Donny and Marie:

- Donny and Marie were well known in America. Most Americans thought Pink Lady was a blended drink.

- Donny and Marie had sold millions of albums in the United States, sung in English. Mie and Kei had sold millions of albums in Japan. In Japanese.

Still, these problems were difficult, not insurmountable. After all, the Monkees couldn't even play instruments when they were prefabricated into a teen-idol rock band. But there was one more small fly in the ointment. A fly the size of a brontosaurus. . . .

• Donny and Marie   Pink Lady couldn't.
  could speak
  English.

At least, that was the joke around the television industry. The women could undoubtedly speak *some* English, and just as undoubtedly understand *some* of it. Unfortunately, what they could speak didn't come out too clearly; listening to Pink Lady try to express themselves in English was something like listening to a friendly sushi chef as he earnestly attempted to communicate a particularly exotic special of the day.

This mangling of the mother tongue may not have kept Charo from American stardom, but NBC realized that Mie and Kei could hardly carry a variety show on their own. Soon the title *Pink Lady* was history, and Tartikoff and Silverman were busily promoting their new show: *Pink Lady and Jeff.*

Jeff was Jeff Altman, a young comedian who had been a regular on two other short-lived series: *Cos* and *The Starland Vocal Band Show.* Altman was ostensibly signed on as the women's sidekick, but he ended up acting as more of an interpreter.

Here's how it worked. The all-American boy, decked out in what looked like a Vegas wedding chapel tuxedo, would crack a joke. Then Mie or Kei would tweak his nose and attempt a Sonny and Cher-ish sort of putdown. Then the laugh track would go nuts while the audience at home cleaned their ears with Q-Tips and debated the meaning of what Mie (or Kei) might have said.

NBC, making the best of what was obviously going to be a bloodbath, debuted *Pink Lady and Jeff* with a one-hour special on Saturday, March 1, 1980, before throwing it to the critical lions in its Friday night time slot.

And what the critics did to *Pink Lady and Jeff* was positively un-Christian. The insipid title of the show drew an opening salvo of jeering and brickbats. Then there was Mie and Kei's misappropriation of the language, which the producers had decided to turn into a running gag about malapropisms. Like two sweetly smiling Oriental versions of Norm Crosby, the women would use some word incorrectly, and the high jinks were supposed to begin.

The costumes were about as hip as the comedy. Altman's standard garb was the aforementioned Wayne Newton tux, but poor Mie and Kei found themselves squeezed into revealing outfits that looked like Linda Blair's hand-me-downs from *Roller Boogie.*

One typically appalling outfit seemed drawn from the wardrobes of about five other characters on other shows. It consisted of a *Wonder*

Mie and Kie—Pink Lady—proved to be a pair of Tokyo Roses for NBC when the network hired them to host a variety hour, à la Donny and Marie, only to discover that the women's grasp of English made Charo seem like Edwin Newman. *NBC*

Woman sort of top with hot pants and wristlets, dotted with both sequins and stripes. It was accessorized with a pair of *Rocky Horror Show* fishnet stockings, and topped off with a sailor collar. Each collar sported a large cursive monogram—M and K—like the ones Penny Marshall wore on *Laverne & Shirley*. If Mr. Blackwell left these particular togs off his annual Worst Dressed list, it could only have been from sheer speechlessness.

Within days, it became clear that if Americans wanted their rock music Pink, they'd listen to Floyd. After only a month on the air (but what felt like a year of stinging embarrassment to NBC), *Pink Lady and Jeff* was ignominiously yanked. *The Rockford Files*, the well-respected James Garner show that had been removed from the schedule to make room for NBC's comedic Pearl Harbor, was hastily rescheduled in its place.

Brandon Tartikoff escaped from this bomb so unscathed that it was nothing short of a miracle. It had never really been his baby in the first place, however; it was all Fred Silverman's abortion.

If *Supertrain* was the first nail in Silverman's million-dollar NBC coffin, *Pink Lady* was the last. His final hope came with the 1980 Moscow Olympics, two weeks of spectacular sports action that belonged solely to NBC. When President Carter withdrew the American teams from competition and the Soviets then withdrew any rights to coverage, NBC was stuck with two weeks of nothing to show. The time was eventually filled with reruns and grade-Z material that had been languishing on the network shelves, but ABC and CBS had wisely counterprogrammed the Olympic Games with some ratings-buster specials. For those two weeks, NBC drew the sort of Nielsens usually associated with public-access Celebrity Bowling.

That was the end of an NBC career for the Man with the Golden Gut, who was transmogrifying into the Guy with the Rusted Belly. Jeff Altman retained some of the powder burns from *Pink Lady*'s detonation, but the comedian went on to spend a year as resident funnyman on the syndicated dance program *Solid Gold*. From there, it was on to regular appearances on *Late Night with David Letterman*, and a 1986 special with Rodney Dangerfield entitled *It's Not Easy Being Me*.

It couldn't have been easy being Pink Lady, either. After the failure of the show, the two promptly returned to American obscurity and flew back to Japan, with the briefest of *sayonaras* for Silverman. They shouldn't feel too bad—after all, the Village People didn't last much longer, either.

Fridays

ABC: 1980–1982

Remember that late-night comedy show that everyone used to watch on the weekends? The one where they got away with salty language and suggestive sketches? The one that took place in front of a live audience, filmed on a weatherbeaten stage, featuring a cast of repertory comedians, guest hosts, and rock music acts?

The one that was on—*Friday* night?

The show that ABC hoped its viewers (and NBC) would lose sleep over was *Fridays*, perhaps the most blatant imitation of a successful show ever put on the air. Like NBC's hit, which came "live, from New York!" every week, *Fridays* came live—from Los Angeles. Like *SNL*, *Fridays* patted itself on the back for being hip, mod, and liberal; and like *SNL*, *Fridays* had an all-white cast with one black guy who was usually relegated to playing jivey dudes and Rastafarians. Then too, rumors of the prodigious ingestion of illegal pharmaceuticals on the sets of both shows

kept the industry talking—and the networks uncomfortable.

The major difference was that *Saturday Night Live* took chances: often misfiring with long, deadening sketches, often scoring fresh satirical hits. *Fridays*, on the other hand, seemed like calculated outrageousness, would-be hip humor spun out of 100 percent virgin polyester.

ABC could hardly deny the similarities between the two shows. "We wouldn't be on the air without *Saturday Night Live*," admitted Jack Burns, *Fridays'* host, coproducer, script supervisor, and creative consultant. "I cannot imagine that when Ford built a successful car that Chevrolet would say, 'Oh well, they've built the car, no sense in us doing it.'"

An odd analogy, to be sure; and certainly television has always found rip-off to be the sincerest form of flattery. But *Fridays'* "borrowing" didn't stop with only the concept. *SNL* had a parody newscast? *Fridays* did too. *SNL* had a purposely rough, unstructured patina? So did *Fridays*.

At that rate, it wouldn't have been surprising to tune in some Friday night to find an actress tackling the original character of "Baba Wawa," or find the cast decked out as Killer Wasps. Sadly, though, the only thing that *Fridays* didn't manage to cadge from *Saturday Night Live* were the laughs.

Fridays scored well on its debut, primarily due to the fact that it *did* fill a need. There was a large untapped audience of young people home on Friday nights (the same audience that, it was hoped, would respond to *Thicke of the Night*). Young people only had the aged *Midnight Special* music program on NBC, which was about as hip and contemporary as Guy Lombardo; when American teenagers were discovering the Sex Pistols and the Ramones, *Midnight Special*'s idea of cutting-edge guests were Barry Manilow and Helen Reddy. Nor did the average fourteen-year-old want to watch a recycled *McMillan and Wife*, even if it was dressed up as "a *CBS Late Movie*."

Critics were lukewarm about the prospect of such a blatant imitation of a highly successful show, but *Fridays* had a lock on the late-night teen market. Musical guests like the Boomtown Rats, Devo, Warren Zevon, and the Jam also brought in the viewers, since these musicians weren't likely to be found on the end of the Carson couch. And *Fridays'* willingness to

book the acts that teenagers wanted to see was often the only thing that kept people watching. When the Clash guest-starred on the show, half the studio audience left after their last song, although *Fridays* still had a while to run.

Still, no stars emerged from *Fridays* the way they had from *SNL*. John Roarke's skillful impression of Ronald Reagan cropped up week after week, but the material was unfalteringly lame; after Roarke said, "Weeeelllll," there really wasn't anywhere to go with the sketches. Melanie Chartoff, an attractive woman with a chilly demeanor, anchored *Fridays'* "Friday Edition" newscast, but she never caught on the way that the attractive-but-chilly Jane Curtin did when she anchored *Saturday Night Live*'s "Weekend Update."

That left shock: a cheap way of getting laughs, but better than none. The initial telecast raised hackles with two skits: a takeoff on *Night of the Living Dead* entitled "Diner of the Living Dead," and an oh-so-wacky feature called "Women Who Spit." After a look at the debut telecast, six ABC affiliates promptly dropped the show and replaced it with their own programming, while others shoved it farther back into the wee hours of the night.

There was another regular source of humor on *Fridays*: drug jokes. Comedians know that the easiest way to wring a laugh out of a recalcitrant audience is to invoke the magical term "Quaalude," and *Fridays* would frequently resort to dopey dope jokes when nothing else would get the audience going. Darrow Igus, *Fridays'* tokenish answer to *SNL's* tokenish Garrett Morris, had a recurring role as a Rastafarian gourmet whose favorite spice was—surprise!—*ganja*. By far the most popular recurring character on the show, though, was The Pharmacist, a pill-popping pill pusher played by Mark Blankfield. Tanked up on what appeared to be equal doses of cocaine, amphetamines, and crystal meth, The Pharmacist's *schtick* was always the same—trying to complete some mundane task while shaking and repeating, "I can handle it. I can handle it." The sketch always got laughs from the fourteen-year-old heavy metal headbangers in the audience, and was indicative of *Fridays'* wit in general—that is, it made Cheech and Chong look like Noel Coward.

Blankfield insisted that the character appealed to all age groups. "The age range of people who have responded to this character has been from nine years old to seventy-six. I knew the children were laughing at the physical things. But the older people are getting into the chemical maintenance of it. I think The Pharmacist is the next evolution in a push-button society." Uh. Yeah.

In the face of continued widespread disinterest, the show began resorting to some desperate tactics to be noticed, like a child screaming its lungs out to get someone, anyone, to pay attention. The first attempt to stir up a synthetic controversy came on the February 20, 1981, show, when Dadaist comedian Andy Kaufman was the guest host.

On the newsmaking telecast, a typically unfunny sketch began to unravel at the seams in what looked to some like a live, unplanned disintegration—and to others like a rehearsed bit. Kaufman, breaking character in a skit set in a restaurant, doused another actor with a glass of water, setting off a brawl. Stagehands and grips entered from off camera to break it up, one of them calling, "Bobby, call a commercial, man!"

Spontaneous? Sure.

When they returned from the commercial, man, Kaufman was still being restrained in the background while cast member Brandis Kemp closed the show by thanking "the portion of Andy Kaufman who was with us tonight."

People took the bait, and *Fridays* received a slew of free publicity when reporters and others called ABC to find out whether the bit was planned or unplanned. The network staunchly insisted that it was a planned bit of Pirandello theater, as anyone who hadn't been snacking on a Rasta Chef recipe could tell, but the ensuing speculation did garner some cheap media attention.

Among the few blows that *Fridays*

landed was an uppercut to the jaw of the *Midnight Special;* the Nielsen ratings showed that the 18–34 age group was deserting the geriatric music program in droves and coming over to *Fridays*. This migration, combined with the new cast on *Saturday Night Live* (which, at times, made *Fridays* look funny), resulted in *Fridays* catching *SNL* in the ratings. Ad rates at *SNL* subsequently plunged to half the levels NBC enjoyed when Gilda Radner et al. were on board, and *Fridays* began winning by default.

Though things were rosy for a while, *Fridays'* ratings soon began to go to pot. The reason: Ted Koppel's *Nightline*, the excellent news program that had preceded *Fridays* throughout most of its run. *Nightline* did so well that the network announced plans to add a one-hour block of news at midnight, Mondays through Fridays, pushing the air time of *Fridays* back to one A.M. And that decision made the ABC Entertainment Center into Bleak House— especially since the cast and crew of the comedy show found out the news by reading about it in *Variety*.

Meanwhile, another show had done what ABC had counted on *Fridays* to accomplish, gathering critical raves and attracting a strong core audience. The show was *SCTV*, ninety minutes of comedy that had begun as a syndicated show imported from Canada. With a cast of improvisational theater veterans drawn from the Second City comedy troupe, *SCTV* skewered the television business with excellent writing and acting. NBC picked up the show and began broadcasting it in the time period left vacant by the departure of the *Midnight Special*, and for fans of late-night comedy, *SCTV* had become the thing to watch on Friday nights.

ABC decided to give *Fridays* a chance to prove itself before consigning the show to the Old Jokes Home. In April 1982 the network slotted the program in for a prime-time "special," opposite a *Dallas* repeat and NBC's *Chicago Story*. The special would be on tape instead of produced live.

Two of the nine cast members bailed out before the pilot was shot, apparently feeling that *Fridays* had become a sinking ship. The remainder of the cast pulled together as plans were made for the make-it-or-break-it telecast. To increase the chances of success, Tony Geary (who was then a hot commodity due to his role on *General Hospital*) was brought in as guest host, and heavy hitters Stevie Wonder and Paul McCartney came aboard to perform their anthem of racial-harmony smarm, "Ebony and Ivory." The rest of the show was filled with the characters that seemed to work best with the late-night audience, making the prime-time show a "*Fridays'* Greatest Hits" package.

The show went well; it didn't beat the *Dallas* rerun, but it did better than the network expected, and

ABC indicated that there was a possibility that *Fridays* might appear in its upcoming fall lineup for 1982–83.

It didn't happen. Come fall, *The Greatest American Hero* went up against the formidable *Dallas*, and *Fridays* malingered on in its late-night time slot until October, when networks began to discover that the MTV-crazed teenagers of the nation would watch inexpensive music video programs all night. *Fridays*, though, was later syndicated, and in one of television's ironies, was picked up by some NBC affiliates to air at 1 A.M. Sunday mornings—right after *Saturday Night Live*, the show that spawned it all. It was all too fitting; the humor that had seemed so sharp and daring on the 1975 *SNL* had grown stale and tired by the early 1980s, and by then the sketches on the former competitors seemed like endless carbon copies of each other. Ironically, it was hard to tell which one was the original.

Hee Haw

CBS: 1969–1971
SYNDICATED: 1971–

Fiddle playin', purty gals, and ancient one-liners were the major export of Kornfield Kounty, the Hicksville *Twilight Zone* from which *Hee Haw* supposedly originated. It was a potent combination that sent critics scrambling for the channel changer, but kept audiences pickin' and a-grinnin' for years and years.

When CBS debuted *Hee Haw* in 1969, it seemed to be a bucolic answer to *Rowan & Martin's Laugh-In*, set in a strange netherland where one's mother was just as likely to be one's sister. Hosted by popular country-western musicians Roy Clark and Buck Owens, *Hee Haw* passed over the flower power movement in favor of good old-fashioned corn power. It was even filmed in Nashville, free of any influence by the CBS Television City slickers.

Like *Laugh-In*, *Hee Haw* was a rapid-fire montage of jokes and music, all tied together by the antics of an animated, buck-toothed donkey whose distinctive bray provided the title for the show. The regulars were a mixed bag of types, all of whom seemed to have escaped from some dinner-theater production of *Li'l Abner*, including the jumbo-economy-sized "Junior" Samples and "Little Lulu" Roman—whose formidable figure was squeezed into a teensy ruffled polka-dot frock. Then there were the personalities familiar from the Nashville tune circuit: Sheb "Purple People Eater" Wooley, Roy Acuff, and Minnie Pearl, whose trademark "Howww-deeee!" could call the hogs in six counties.

Another staple of *Hee Haw* was the beautiful girl-next-door types, many of whom happened to be associated with famous men. There was Linda (Mrs. Bruce) Jenner, Marianne (Mrs. Kenny) Rogers, and Barbi Benton, who had gone from life as a UCLA coed to life as Hugh Hefner's snugglebunny in record time. These regulars were tossed in a crazy salad with assorted good ole boys, washboard players, country cousins, hicks of all descriptions, and George a.k.a. "Goober" Lindsay, swapping

Preacherman Billy Graham was among the guest who dropped by *Hee Haw* during its long run. Getting sage counsel from the reverend are George "Goober" Lindsey, left, and "Grandpa" Jones.

Hee Haw wants you, says George "Goober" Lindsey. Millions of Americans tuned in every week for the show's combination of cornpone humor and cheatin' heart music.

farmer's-daughter jokes and square dancing their way through each telecast.

It wasn't Cole Porter, but it filled a need for a lot of rural viewers who were often ignored by the supposed sophisticates who control the airwaves. TV watchers, especially in the South, tuned in faithfully each week to "hee-haw" at the korn-fed kuties and listen to the sort of cheatin'-heart tunes that they never heard on *Shindig* or *Soul Train*.

CBS executives, though, had finally had their fill of "rural" programming. Although the shows were exceedingly popular, the network axed *Hee Haw* in a purge that also removed *Green Acres* and *Mayberry R.F.D.* from the schedule—gradually replacing them with more city-oriented comedy like *All in the Family* and *The Mary Tyler Moore Show*.

Hee Haw had proved, however, that it was hip to be square, and it simply do-si-do'd its way into syndication the next year, following the example of that other network-rejected family program, *The Lawrence Welk Show*. In syndication, *Hee Haw* was shown on more stations than it ever was on CBS, and it even beat the network shows in many cities, mostly in the South. Host Roy Clark even cut a record about the achievement: "The Lawrence Welk–*Hee Haw* Counterrevolutionary Polka."

Throughout its long run in syndication, *Hee Haw* managed to attract

United States Senate Majority Leader Robert Byrd offers his rendition of "Turkey in the Straw" in just one of the timeless moments of *Hee Haw* hilarity.

much of Nashville's top talent to stop by for a few songs, including several who became regulars (Slim Pickens, a Mandrell sister or two). *Hee Haw* even drew some unlikely fans—including Senate Majority Leader Robert Byrd, a frustrated fiddle-picker who stopped by the haystack for a rousing rendition of "Turkey in the Straw" on one episode.

Everyone, it seems, either loves or hates *Hee Haw*. Critics screamed and city folks groaned, but *Hee Haw* continued to steamroll its way across the television screens of America for years and years with its mix of homespun humor and moonshine music. The formula worked. As Barbi Benton analyzed the success of the show, "You jump out of the cornfield and get hit by the board fence. You sit in a haystack and make dirty jokes."

It's a logic that seems to have escaped the city slickers that run the networks. One thing's for sure: As long as there's white trash, there'll always be a *Hee Haw*.

Fat City:
The Shows that Squeezed Laughs out of Lard

Audiences have always embraced overweight TV personalities, from Jackie Gleason and Alfred Hitchcock to Benny Hill and Oprah Winfrey. Two of NBC's longest-running sitcoms of the 1980s, in fact, were nicknamed in the industry as *The Fats of Life* and *Gimme a Steak!*, after the expanding waistlines of their popular stars.

Two notable—and short-lived—sitcoms were built around the premise that fat is funny. And while the comical qualities of cellulite are debatable, the alleged comedies on Channel 11 are definitely painful. Pull up a box of Twinkies and an easy chair and tune in.

The Dumplings
NBC: 1976

Weight watchers and chubby chasers all over the United States had their own tailor-made, extra-large sitcom with *The Dumplings*, a two-dimensional show that was, appropriately enough, based on an eponymous comic strip.

The Dumplings was set in a New York luncheonette owned and operated by Joe and Angela Dumpling, a couple whose love for each other was matched only by the size of their waistbands. The show was promoted heavily before its arrival, due to the sterling credits of the actors who would play the porky proprietors: James Coco and Geraldine Brooks.

Coco weighed more than three hundred pounds at times, making him the entertainment industry's leading overweight actor during the 1970s; it seemed that every time a script called for a Jolly Fat Man, Coco was always in the running. His partner, Brooks, was a familiar character actress whose own figure was more sylphlike than gargantuan. She hadn't had a glandular imbalance; Brooks actually weighed in the neigh-

borhood of 110 pounds, which necessitated ingenious use of padding and makeup by the *Dumplings* costumer.

Although the choice of Brooks to play an overweight character might seem on a par with casting James Earl Jones as Archie Bunker, casting a thin woman as a fat woman was only one of the questionable decisions made by Tandem, the Norman Lear company that dreamed up the show. The major one, of course, might have been how anyone could (or would want to) wring laughs out of excess avoirdupois. Still, it was hard to understand how Lear could conceive of a comedy about a blue-collar bigot and his "dingbat" wife; if anyone could make *The Dumplings* funny, Lear was the man for the job.

Woody Allen himself probably couldn't have wrung a chuckle out of the show, however. Compounding the problems in concept was a middling group of supporting characters who would stop by the diner for a cheeseburger or just a cup of coffee and a schmooze: Angela's sister, people who worked in the building, Man-

Coco Puffs: The late James Coco played half of the title role in *The Dumplings,* a feeble sitcom larded with jokes about fat people.

hattan street types. Unlike the gang on *Cheers*, though, or the newsroom types on *The Mary Tyler Moore Show*, they were only cardboard foils for the Dumplings themselves.

And the Dumplings, as played by Coco and Brooks, weren't just comfortable with their weight. They *reveled* in being fat, and all the cutesy-poo blubber-wallowing was enough to send any vaguely paunchy viewer scurrying to Weight Watchers. Worst of all, the sight of them grinding their behemoth behinds together, giggling and smirking as they nuzzled their glutei maximi, was hardly cute—it was a gross-out of the highest order.

Booty-bumping, distasteful as it was, didn't sink the show—especially since the rear ends in question belonged to such talented individuals as Coco and Brooks. It was the parboiled scripts, which would have been lucky to have as much meat on their bones as the Dumplings did.

Part of the problem stemmed from the lead characters' chirpy natures, which was reminiscent of Richard Simmons'—in 48-inch-waist pants. With all this love and happiness, it was hard to give a damn about anything that happened on the show, and the Dumplings' conflicts were as doughy and bland as matzoh balls. When you've got to build a half hour around two people's bubbly attitudes and the fact that a good restaurant review brings them more business than they can handle, you're in trouble. (In a situation like that, butting butts becomes a major plot point.)

Reviews were mixed, concentrating more on the performances than the scripts. *The Wall Street Journal*, however, noted, "It should be recalled by the factory for an overhaul. Once again, the plot sounds like something from a satire of television."

James Coco, as ebullient off camera as he was on, expected the show to be a big hit, but pointed out, "I've been in eight hundred flops that closed in New Haven. So thirteen weeks in a TV series is a long run, baby!"

Too bad (for Coco's sake, at least) that *The Dumplings* didn't even last that long. It debuted on NBC in January 1976, and was gone from the airwaves less than two months later, leaving the actor sadder but wiser. "My best show on *The Dumplings* was never seen because we were preempted by a Ronald Reagan speech!" he groused. It does neither Reagan nor *The Dumplings* credit to speculate as to which would have been more interesting.

Sadly, Brooks was dead within another year, and Coco himself passed away in 1987, so a revival of *The Dumplings* isn't likely unless Raymond Burr and Oprah Winfrey suddenly get the urge to work together. Joe and Angie Dumpling were yanked from the air in March 1976—no doubt sent to a fat farm, because *The Dumplings*, during its brief run, was anything but a funny farm.

One in a Million
ABC: 1980

"Portly Little Rich Girl!" could have been the title for this corpulent sitcom. It starred hefty Shirley Hemphill as a jive-talking, plain-spoken cab driver who becomes the richest woman in the world overnight, turning cries of "Fat, fat, the water rat" into "Fat, fat, the corporate rat."

Hemphill was a former stand-up comedienne who got her first big series break in *What's Happening!!*—a situation comedy that featured not one, not two, but three overweight characters as the butt of fat jokes. As "Shirley," the piggish waitress at the corner diner, Hemphill had plenty of competition in the cellulite category from Fred Berry as a tubby, break-dancing teenager and Mabel King as a behemoth mother. It was a perfect training ground for Hemphill, as most of the terrible jokes on *What's Happening!!* arose from the characters' bulk. ("You'd be a great witness. You could throw yourself on the mercy of the court and smother the jury.")

After *What's Happening!!* bit the dust, Hemphill moved on to a tailor-made vehicle suspiciously reminiscent of the old Judy Holliday flick *The Solid Gold Cadillac*. In *Cadillac*, Holliday played a minority stockholder who brought a major corporation to its knees by embarrassing the industrialists with her own brand of eccentric common sense. Unfortunately, the updating of *Cadillac* for Hemphill's top-heavy talents resulted in an Edsel of a show.

In *One in a Million*, squirrely Shirley played a cabbie who charmed one of her regular riders with her earthy viewpoints. As it turned out, he was a majority stockholder in Grayson Enterprises, a conglomerate that made Beatrice look puny in scope.

The owners of huge corporations rarely depend on cabs to squire them from appointment to appointment, but that minor plot point didn't matter for long on *One in a Million;* the industrialist conveniently died in the first episode, leaving Shirley two hundred million dollars in his will. When she found out, of course, Shirley passed out, leaving the board of directors trying to catch the whale of a gal before she hit the floor.

A nine-figure check like that could buy a lot of Sara Lee cheesecake and Mallomars, but Shirley also had another choice: She could run the company. On Wall Street, this would be about as likely as Clara "Where's the Beef" Peller taking over the Wendy's corporation, but reality on *One in a Million* was dosed out in inverse proportion to the fat jokes. Did Shirley take the money and run, or did she decide to stay on and run Grayson Enterprises with no experience? (Those who thought she went for the long green are hereby remanded to enroll in Remedial Comedy Writing 1A.)

And what does Shirley do? Insider stock trading? Strip-mine national parks? Turn the San Fernando Valley into Love Canal West? No sir-ree, Bob—she decides to become The Voice of the People at Grayson Enterprises, turning the corporation into a socially conscious body doing good work for the average Joe and Josephine.

This scenario rivals that of *My Mother the Car* for plausibility, but ABC thought Hemphill could carry it off—especially if she had a coterie of cardboard villains with silk hats ready to be knocked off the tops of their heads. Unfortunately, all the writers on *One in a Million* could come up with was this sort of blue-collar breast-beating, punctuated by one-liners about Shirley's rotundity.

It wasn't enough to last. Although ABC programmers might have thought that if the public would watch *What's Happening!!*, they'd watch *anything*, the public wasn't willing to buy *One in a Million*. As a colorful supporting character, Shirley made an excellent buffoon, but as a leading lady, she was no Judy Holliday. *One in a Million* was dumped into the schedule as a mid-season replacement in January 1980, and it languished at the bottom of the ratings for two months before being yanked. It returned for a brief run in June before disappearing entirely.

Although she was off television for several years, Hemphill fans were pleased to see her return in *What's Happening Now!!*, an "updating" of the old show with the now-jowly old regulars back to doing what they did best—slinging insults about each other's weight. By then, *One in a Million* was completely forgotten, and Shirley was back in the history books as the fattest fat cat of them all.

Beast Infections:
Those Amazing Animal Shows and Their Maladroit Mammals

Many human stars would be gratified to achieve one-tenth of the limelight that TV's animal stars have basked in over the years. None of Lassie's owners were ever as popular as the famous collie. Other animal actors— Rin-Tin-Tin, Mr. Ed, Alvin and the Chipmunks, and Gentle Ben—have fans every bit as devoted as the boosters of a Tom Selleck or a Linda Evans. Still, a few animal stars never quite caught the fancy of the American public. Channel 12 is currently broadcasting the antics of some deservedly forgotten quadrupeds, all of whom deserved the glue factory for their truly bestial attempts at family entertainment.

Me and the Chimp

CBS: 1972

"This has got to be the giant mistake in my life," moaned Ted Bessell. It was break time on the set of his new series *Me and the Chimp*, and the "Me" of the title was having misgivings. His costar was relaxing in her dressing room, no doubt enjoying a banana or two and reminding herself that Bonzo started this way as well.

Bessell wasn't being temperamental—just prescient. After all, he'd just finished five years of playing Don Hollinger on *That Girl*, the hit sitcom that put Marlo Thomas—and Bessell—on the map. It was Bessell who popped up every time Thomas screwed up her face and yelled, "Donaaaaald!"

After That Sitcom ended, Bessell was, in the words of the *L.A. Times*, "one of the hottest items in town." But after the failure of a surrealistic, innovative pilot, *Bobby Parker and Company*, he found himself casting about for a TV project.

Among the scripts sent his way was a pilot from Garry Marshall and

Tom Miller entitled *The Chimp and I*. With thoughts of J. Fred Muggs, the Marquis Chimps, and *Planet of the Apes* dancing in his head, Miller had wanted to do a program with a monkey. Garry Marshall (who would go on to create *Happy Days*, *Laverne & Shirley*, and *Mork & Mindy*) had fleshed out the storyline: A man who hates animals is forced to live with a chimpanzee.

"I threw it in the back of my car without reading it," remembered Bessell, but his agent rescued it and badgered his client to put aside any aversions to the script and just do it. "I don't like shows like that. I don't like Lassie or Flipper. I don't even like wives and kids!," moaned Bessell. Eventually, against his better judgment, he chose *Chimp* out of six possible script offers.

The resulting sixteen-minute test film was flown to New York for the thumbs-up or thumbs-down of one very important CBS programming executive—the legendary Fred Silverman. CBS was getting creamed

Ted Bessell (bottom) got up to many hilarious high jinks with Buttons the chimp (top) on *Me and the Chimp*.

on Thursday nights, due to the unexpected popularity of *The Flip Wilson Show*, which was making any attempt at counterprogramming almost superfluous. Silverman saw *The Chimp and I* as a chance to muscle in on Flip Wilson by capturing the kiddie audience; after all, Geraldine shouting "The devil made me do it!" didn't hold much appeal for a first-grader. The sight of a chimpanzee making a mess in the kitchen, however, was certain to crack up the six-year-olds—and the adults with six-year-old mentalities. As Silverman put it, he thought that the program would "make the whole country chimp-conscious."

Before long, it became all too clear to Ted Bessell that he was being made *chump*-conscious, forced to play second banana (as it were) to a monkey. One industry joke had it that he refused to do the show until the title was switched from *The Chimp and I* to *Me and the Chimp*—working with a chimp was one thing, but taking second billing to one was another. Whether or not the story was true, it was the last indignity that Bessell would be spared on the show.

He played Dr. Mike Reynolds, a dentist whose two hyperadorable children discover a chimpanzee hiding out in a playground drainpipe and bring the animal home—to the delight of their mother and the chagrin of Dr. Mike. But uh-oh, the chimp has escaped from an Air Force research center, and he's been trained to press buttons—all kinds of buttons, and the automotively destructive chimp is soon named Buttons.

Because of monkeys' mercurial natures, Buttons soon had the set of *Me and the Chimp* wrapped around his ugly little finger. When Buttons was ready to shoot, they shot. When he wasn't, they didn't.

Actually, Buttons was played by a chimp named Jackie. And, in a twist on *Lassie* (where a male collie played a female), Jackie was a female chimp playing a male. This bit of trans-monkeyshines made no difference to Bessell, and soon the two were exhibiting more mutual antipathy than any costars since Nelson Eddy and Jeanette MacDonald, with Bessell even telling columnists that Buttons was "rude, dirty, and untalented.

"I don't care for the chimp," he complained to a visitor on the set as Buttons bounced up and down in her own little canvas chair. "This has got to be the giant mistake in my life. . . . That monkey is a savage. For six million years, the monkeys of the world have been working up to this show. If we can get canceled in thirteen weeks, my life might be saved."

Bob Riedell, Jackie/Buttons' trainer, defended his client, who was pulling in a cool thousand dollars a week. "This is nerve-wracking, an ulcer job," Riedell said. "She gets along fine with Ted. How he gets along with her—you'll have to ask him."

"I'm tired of all the puddles on the set," was Bessell's reply. "I've ruined three pairs of shoes already."

The only people who knew how to push Bessell's buttons better than the chimp were the critics, who thought the show had a missing link in the humor department. "This is a show on two levels," said *TV Guide*, "ours and the chimp's. On the chimp's level, it's terrific.... The idea of the show is apparently his." After debuting in third place, below *Alias Smith and Jones* and well below *The Flip Wilson Show*, *Me and the Chimp* continued to sink in the ratings until its cancellation four months later—when it was pulling in about half the tiny audience it enjoyed on its debut.

"Everybody tells me," groused Bessell, "that if the show's a hit, it's because of the chimp; if it flops, it's my fault."

Bingo. Tom Tannenbaum, head of production at Paramount, finally had had it with the griping of his human star. "We had concept problems," said Tannenbaum. "Bessell saw it one way, we saw it another. He felt he should always be against the chimp staying in his house, while everybody else wanted the chimp to stay. I think the chimp should have stayed and Bessell should have left."

Apparently Ted felt the same way. He subsequently retired from acting for two years, resurfacing on Broadway. The further career moves of Jackie, however, have never been pinned down; although she would have been perfect in the title role when *Planet of the Apes* became a weekly series in 1974, that role went to Roddy McDowall instead.

Skippy, the Bush Kangaroo

SYNDICATED: 1969–1971

Boing!   Boing!   Boing!

There's trouble afoot, and a heroic animal is on its way to right a wrong and ensure that good triumphs over evil. Here comes salvation from the wild kingdom. It's no heroic collie in the Lassie mold. It's not Corporal Rusty and Private Rin-Tin-Tin. (Yo, Rinty!) It's not even Boomer, that NBC dog star whose series *Here's Boomer* established him as the canine Jayne Mansfield next to the true Marilyn Monroe of the kennel, Benji. Nope, our hero here is Skippy, the fearless Bush Kangaroo herself, hopping her way across the outback straight into your heart.

Clearly, producer Lee Robinson thought that a brave kangaroo would be the successor to all the beloved animal stars listed above. Perhaps Robinson even envisioned a generation of American kiddies sporting kangaroo-skin caps as proudly as their older siblings had worn coonskin chapeaux in the 1950s. After all, hadn't the whole country gone around humming "Tie Me Kangaroo Down, Sport" just a few years before?

In retrospect, there were thousands of other animals that might have been better candidates for a marsupial hero. A thorough look at modern children's literature reveals only two kangaroos who achieved any sort of fame: Winnie the Pooh's pals Kanga and Roo, who were at best mere supporting players to Pooh, Piglet, Eeyore, and the gang.

Then there was the problem of naming the 'roo. "Skippy" was bound to ensure snorts of derision from adults, who certainly didn't want aid arriving in the persona of a marsupial named after a jar of peanut butter. (Then again, maybe it wasn't such a bad choice; "Vegemite, the Bush Kangaroo" is even worse.)

Like *Daktari*, *Skippy* was set on a game preserve in an exotic locale—Australia, naturally. And where *Daktari*'s denizens included some truly exciting wild animals, like lions and tigers (but no bears, oh my), *Skippy*'s breathtaking adventures held no more danger than a cuddle with a koala.

The series was filmed on location in Australia's Waratah National Park, where Ranger Hammond and his little boy Sonny protected the outback. Sonny, who apparently didn't have the patience to tame a platypus or a wildebeest, spends his days playing with Skippy, a domesticated female kangaroo who often helps the Hammonds in their quest for Truth, Justice, and the Australian Way.

All this was presented to the world's children by Kellogg's, obviously in the hope that Skippy and her exploits would provide the perfect counterpoint to a mouthful of Frosted Flakes on Saturday morning television. The series was reasonably popular, racking up over 90 episodes in the late sixties and forming the basis for a small, dedicated cult of strange children who preferred Skippy's kickboxing style to the far more genteel Lassie.

The show also provided a small measure of fame for its stars, most of whom went on from *Skippy* to languish in obscurity. Ed Devereaux, the Australian actor who played Ranger Hammond, had toiled for decades in the entertainment industry, only to find that *Skippy* provided him with the recognition he had long sought. In an interview years later, Devereaux remembered, "I *still* get people singing the theme song to me in the streets. I don't mind."

Looking back on the entire *Skippy* experience, though, it's clear that the problem with the hopping hero wasn't the blatant stupidity of the whole premise; after all, there have been far worse shows for children, including *Rubik, the Amazing Cube,* an animated series about a cube that rolled around performing good deeds. The trouble with *Skippy* was merely being ahead of its time. With Australiamania sweeping America in the eighties, wouldn't it be a perfect time to give *Skippy, the Bush Kangaroo* a facelift and a revival? Guest stars like Paul Hogan and Judy Davis could drop by Waratah National Park to banter with the Pouched One, and Olivia Newton-John could rerecord the evergreen *Skippy* theme. Even the Qantas Airlines bear, that symbol of Aussie tourism, could make a cameo appearance as Skippy's koala pal. And if all this failed, Skippy could always team up with Mel Gibson for a *Road Warrior* sequel entitled *Hopping Mad Max.*

Manimalia at NBC

If At First You Don't Succeed . . .

MAN FROM ATLANTIS: 1977–1978
MANIMAL: 1983
MISFITS OF SCIENCE: 1984

How did NBC transform from schlock network (*The Montefuscos, Who's Watching the Kids?*, *Grandpa Goes to Washington*) to a class act? By switching to a format of clever comedies and innovative dramas like *The Golden Girls* and *L.A. Law*. Long before these triumphs, though network executives kept reworking one "high concept" in an attempt to find some success with a patently stupid idea, apparently with the adage "If at first you don't succeed, flop, flop again" in mind.

For several years, NBC executives became fascinated by the notion of a superhero with extraordinary powers; unlike *Batman* or *Superman*, though, NBC's thoroughly mod superheroes were played totally straight. Apparently the network executives assumed that the bohunks who populated the American breadbasket wouldn't have their intelligence strained—or insulted—by a Gill-Man from Atlantis, or a rock star who shoots lightning bolts from his fists. Each time, the network was proven wrong when the latest preposterous series sank like a stone; each time, NBC tried, tried again. If not for *The Cosby Show*, they might never have stopped trying.

The first attempt at capturing the attention of Americans with arrested IQs came in 1977, with the debut of *Man from Atlantis*. For the sensitive role of the half-human, half-fish Gill-Man, the network chose an unknown actor by the name of Patrick Duffy.

As the title character in NBC's soggy saga, Duffy had little to do but look hairlessly hunky in the underwater scenes and seem benignly puzzled by the scientists who wanted to examine him. Naturally, it would certainly have been inconvenient (and expensive) if the earthbound scientists had to spend all their time beneath the waves to communicate with Duffy, so the writers decided that he could breathe air for short periods of time. Best of all, the intense water pressure at the bottom of the ocean had given Duffy superhuman strength, resulting in a sort of Bionic Mackerel.

Aquabeefcake: Patrick Duffy played the sensitive title character in *The Man from Atlantis*. Note the ludicrously fake "webbing" between his fingers, as well as the visible vaccination scar on his left bicep. Apparently even gill-men have to protect against measles.

The network wanted to give *Atlantis* every chance to float in the sink-or-swim ratings world; four "pre-episodes" were broadcast before the program made its actual debut in September, and beefcake photographs of Patrick Duffy—hair wet, shirtless—were liberally distributed to the media. (Although residents of Atlantis no doubt swam about their daily business sans benefit of bathing suits, NBC wasn't ready to irk the censors for the sake of authenticity; Duffy was always modestly clad. Besides, any air of reality in *Man from Atlantis* might just have killed the entire series.)

One would think that the prospect of a Gill-Man hunk traveling in a supersubmarine with a team of American scientists would provide quite enough intrigue for boneheaded plots, but the writers on *Man from Atlantis* seemed to run out of ideas immediately. Therefore, the Gill-Man and the scientists began to find themselves in situations that were distinctly fishy: Duffy and company even began traveling in time (through those well-known "undersea time portals"), as well as dealing with extraterrestrial life.

Man from Atlantis dog-paddled its way through a full year on the network before hitting deep water. Patrick Duffy must have been happy to discover that his career wasn't all washed up; shortly after *Atlantis* left the air, he went on to costar in *Dallas*. When he decided to leave the show and his character, Bobby, was killed off, *Dallas* seemed to lose its compass, and the public outcry was so great that he returned to the show with one of the most outrageous conceits ever to take place in a soap opera: The writers wrote off an entire season of shows (from Duffy's death to his "resurrection") as an extended nightmare—his wife, Pam, had simply had a bad dream. It would have taken a lot more than that to resuscitate *Man from Atlantis*, however, which sank beneath the waves in 1978 leaving few regrets.

Undaunted, NBC revived the same theme in 1983 with *Manimal*, a show that was usually described as a cross between a dog and a turkey. Talk about your high concept; *Manimal* seemed to be a mating of *Wild Kingdom* and a sex-change operation.

Manimal was nothing as pedestrian as a mere man-fish. He was a college professor named Jonathan Chase (Simon MacCorkindale) who could transform himself into any creature at will. His powers apparently came from his father, "sole heir to the secret link that binds man and animal," whose travels through Darkest Africa or Darkest South America or Darkest Cleveland had left him with the power to perform transspecies surgery on himself.

Criminals, of course, never suspected that the puppy dogging their heels was actually a Ph.D. working for the police, and more than one

No, it's not a *Dallas* outtake. Patrick Duffy, a water-breathing alien from the lost continent of Atlantis, is magically transported through a time warp to the Old West. *NBC*

ne'er-do-well must have wondered where in the hell that pouncing tiger came from. The Manimal's usual guise, however, was a penguin—due to the fact that MacCorkindale's male model looks filled out a tuxedo so nicely.

Although a man who could change himself into a serpent or a rogue elephant wouldn't seem to need much help with his life, the Manimal did have a couple of pals who helped him crack cases when he wasn't grading papers. Professor Chase was assisted by a beautiful blonde police detective, who took his transformations in stride; apparently working the streets of Manhattan can inure a cop to even the most unusual of situations. The two worked with Ty, a character who must have been drawn from that Central Casting file marked Jive-Talking, Streetwise Black Dude.

NBC debuted *Manimal* in September 1983 as part of a Friday evening lineup touted as highly as the *Cosby–Family Ties–Cheers–Night Court* slate on Thursdays. *Manimal*'s compatriots in brain death were *Jennifer Slept Here* (an Ann Jillian sitcom about a curvaceous ghost) and *Mr. Smith*, a comedy about a talking orangutan that advised the government on defense matters.

"*Mr. Smith* could be the breakout show of 1983. So could *Manimal*," said Brandon Tartikoff, president of NBC's entertainment division. Tartikoff's faith in the strength of *Manimal* was so strong, in fact, that he scheduled it against *Dallas* on CBS. Predictably, the transmammal was no match for J.R. Ewing, and the ratings looked as dismal as the show's premise. While *Jennifer Slept Here* finished 56th out of 70 shows, and *Mr. Smith* held down the 59th position, poor *Manimal* was mired at number 63. When the first week of December rolled around, NBS canceled nearly all of its new shows, and *Manimal* was last aired on the last day of 1983.

If there's one certainty in the TV industry, it's that executives never learn from their mistakes. Two years later, *Dallas* continued its imperious reign in the Friday-at-9 time slot, with NBC's *Hunter* proving to be ineffectual in its attempts to knock off Larry Hagman's famous Stetson. Reaching back to *Manimal* and *Man from Atlantis*, NBC came up with another 'M' show to attempt to blunt *Dallas*.

The show was *Misfits of Science*, and it attempted to succeed with *more* superheroes who had *more* superpowers, in a premise that was even *more* superstupid than *Manimal* or *Atlantis*. To the network's credit, *Misfits* was billed as a "humorous adventure" or "comedy adventure" series.

After all, it's hard not to laugh when you're faced with a crimefighting team like the one assembled by a crusading scientist played by the late Dean Paul Martin. Especially when his chief operative is yet another "Jive-Talking, Streetwise Black Dude"—the major difference between this fellow and Ty from *Manimal* being that this "J.-T. S.B.D." was 7'4" tall. Oh, yes—this fellow could also shrink to a height of 6 inches at will, which would make him the ideal crime fighter should Malibu Barbie ever decide to knock over a bank.

The team also included a guy named Beef, who could freeze anything he wanted to by simply touching it. Whenever one of the Misfits should query, "Where's the Beef?," he would most likely be found inside a nearby refrigerator, where he lived.

Almost plausible in comparison was Johnny B, a rock star who possessed the unique ability to shoot bolts of electricity from his fists at will. And to top things off, Dean Paul had his ace in the hole, a pretty teenager with *Carrie*like telekinetic powers. The girl was played by Courtney Cox, an aspiring actress whose star rose brightly and briefly in 1985 with a one-minute role in Bruce Springsteen's "Dancing in the Dark" video. NBC might as well have named

Misfits of Science was one of NBC's attempts to achieve the success that had eluded *The Man from Atlantis* and *Manimal*. With the late Dean Paul Martin (lower right) in charge, the misfits provided an embarrassing few months for the peacock network. *NBC*

the show *The Odd Squad.*

These characters might have been a hit if they were produced in bad Japanese animation and presented on Saturday morning television as filler between Count Chocula ads, but as a prime-time competitor to *Dallas,* the positioning was pretty pathetic. "It looks like Brandon Tartikoff is just going to keep doing *Manimal* until he gets it right," sneered TV critic Elvis Mitchell.

It might have come as a surprise to NBC entertainment executives, but it was no great shock to anyone else when the *Misfits of Science* proved to be the misfits of the fall season and were among the first shows axed by the now-dominant network.

Misfits' abject failure, it seemed, might have taught a lesson to the ivory tower types at NBC, and there were no superhuman superheroes in the 1986 fall schedule. There was, however, *ALF,* a comedy about an extraterrestrial that comes to live in suburbia—and the show's resemblance to its obvious spiritual fathers, *Atlantis* and *Manimal,* wasn't a coincidence. The network had merely thrown an *E.T.* spin on the old warhorse and come up with a poor puppet version of a superhero. (*ALF* looked like a Muppet on acid and spoke like an interplanetary Buddy Hackett.)

Thankfully, audiences bought none of this nonsense, but TV executives have never been known for learning from their mistakes. Any day now, NBC might attempt a weekly version of that old favorite, *I Was a Teenage Werewolf.* Is Simon MacCorkindale available?

CHANNEL 13

The Lame Games:
Humiliation on the Game Show Circuit

TV programmers love game shows. They're cheap, easy to produce, and can provoke a fanatical reaction in ardent fans. News directors who spend millions to lure a Tom Brokaw or Peter Jennings to anchor the news—might do better instead if they simply gave up and hired Bob Barker to read the headlines.

The vast majority of game shows don't demand any great knowledge; while a few brainy programs like *Jeopardy!* might require familiarity with European history or the works of Shakespeare, the average show's prime prerequisite is a toothy smile and the ability to jump up and down like a jack-in-the-box on amphetamines.

A double-digit IQ and the ability to make an ass of oneself on camera were all that was needed to score points—and make money—on the game shows currently being seen on Channel 13.

Queen for a Day

NBC: 1955–1959
ABC: 1959–1964

"I now pronounce you—Queen for a Day!"

For twenty years on radio and TV, those words would transform Hannah the Housewife into a cheapjack Grace Kelly. They were also NBC's ticket to Number One status in the daytime TV market, and, to students of macabre broadcasting, the first faint stirrings of what would one day become the formula for Chuck Barris's string of programming pearls.

Queen began on radio in 1945, providing vicarious thrills for the public and outraging the critics. When it made the transition from audio to video on New Year's Day 1955, though, it became one of daytime television's biggest—and most lucrative—hits, playing on the sympathy and voyeurism of its largely female audience.

"And just because of its phenomenal commercial and popular success," wrote the show's producer, Howard Blake, in 1966, "a close look at this program, I am convinced, reveals with shining clarity the essential, sobering truth about radio and TV in these United States."

If true, the picture is grim. Each episode of *Queen* began with longtime host Jack Bailey looking straight at the home audience and asking the obvious question: *"Would you like to be Queen for a Day?"*

Ah, but the road to the throne was as treacherous as any in Roman history. Pretenders to the title were selected from each day's live audience, in much the same way as *The Price Is Right* is cast, and each lady entering the arena was given a "wish card," on which she could elaborate on her pathetic circumstances and describe the object that would be the answer to her prayers.

After the show's producer narrowed the wish card selection down to an easy two dozen or so, Bailey would call the semifinalists onto the stage for a brief pre-interview, selecting the ones with the best, most pathetic, most emotionally overwrought stories to tell. By the time

Queen for a Day host Jack Bailey and the show's leggy models, Carol Anders and Maxine Reeves (the 1954 prototypes of Vanna White), get ready for the show's national TV debut on the NBC network. *NBC*

the cameras rolled, only the top five remained onstage, while the other candidates were ushered back to the audience to watch the proceedings.

The show began with a parade of consumer goods, happily donated by manufacturers eager to obtain such prize commercial time. The captains of industry even *paid* for the privilege, covering the cost of many of the salaries involved with the show. Each day featured an embarrassment of riches that would put Vanna White and her never-ending stream of "fabulous and exciting merchandise" to shame.

Going from luxury to heartache, five sob sisters would tell their tales, often through teary eyes that were expertly milked by the sympathetically simpering Jack Bailey. (Bailey, not uncoincidentally, had spent time as both a department store salesman and a carnival barker.)

And then, as the women stood mere feet away from the dowry promised them by Jack Bailey, it was time for the voting. While *Queen for a Day* was a monarchy, the voting procedure was purely democratic instead of inherited. It was the *audience*—the fellow voyeurs and the would-be queens—that decided who would become their ruler.

This was accomplished by a gadget that became the butt of comedians' jokes for years to come, and was used twenty years later to break ties on *The Gong Show*. It was the applause meter, and, just so no one at home would feel left out, it would appear on the screen while the audience clapped their ballot choices.

"I now pronounce you—Queen for a Day!" screamed Bailey at the end of the voting, while the cameras zeroed in on that day's queen, who was usually awash in salt water. The cameras had to move quickly, though, since the other potential queens often burst into tears as well; after baring their souls and describing their problems on television, they were only a "parting gift" richer. (Needless to say, a terminally ill woman who needed hospital equipment wasn't likely to be thrilled with a toaster and a handful of cosmetics.)

A new queen was crowned more like a beauty pageant winner than like Elizabeth II, though. A spangled tiara was plopped on her head; a sable-trimmed robe was put around her shoulders; a dozen long-stemmed roses were put in her arms; and Bailey led her to a tacky throne while her gifts were brought before her like labor-saving supplicants. Each show ended with Bailey's famous catchphrase: "Be with us tomorrow when we'll elect another queen. This is Jack Bailey, wishing we could make every woman queen for a day!"

This mixture of Greed and Gutwrenching proved so popular that *Queen* became daytime TV's biggest hit by April, and in July NBC expanded it to a highly unusual 45-minute format. ("Only about 15 of the 45 minutes were left for the ac-

It was *Drag Queen for a Day* when Jack Bailey and Hollywood columnist Jimmy Star outfitted themselves in the finery of America's luckiest housewives. *NBC*

tual show," remembers producer Blake. "The other 30 minutes were nothing more than commercials and plugs.")

The merchandise, of course, fulfilled a lot of air-castle fantasies for American homemakers, but it was really the tales of woe that got them tuning in every day. A selection of the "wish cards" reveals the desperation of the women:

"A bird for an old lady, 94 [sic]. She had one but it died. She does not realize it is dead. She keeps it in a cage, talks to it, takes it out and kisses its head."

"$100 for a divorce. Husband attempted rape on my 6-year-old daughter, then left with money and car. Must be divorced so I can testify against him in court."

"An artificial eye for my husband. Last winter his artificial eye (which he keeps in a small glass at night) froze and cracked. I have 16 children and No. 17 is coming up in the spring."

"The most needy and deserving usually had to be dumped," admits Blake. "A candidate had to want something we could plug—a stove, a carpet, a plane trip, an artificial leg, a detective agency, a year's supply of baby food. And the reason she needed whatever it was had to make a good story. . . . We had only one aim—to pick the woman who would provide the best entertainment."

Network programmers being what they are, *Queen* was soon often imitated but never duplicated. The success of the radio version spawned CBS's *Strike it Rich!*, in which people in crisis would pour out their stories à la *Queen*. The difference on *Rich!* was that sponsors were never involved; the *home audience* supplied the money on the "Heart Line," a telephone bank set up in the Manhattan studio.

Often imitated. Never duplicated. The 1959 transition from NBC to ABC (which would be echoed when the networks swapped *Let's Make a Deal* a decade later) was a chancy move by ABC, but God saved the *Queen*. It kept cranking out royalty until October 1964, when the Queen Machine came to a halt and Jack

Los Angeles, 1978: Jack Bailey reminisced at home about *Queen for a Day.*

Bailey retired after crowning thousands of ersatz regal beagles. As producer Blake put it, "We got what we were after. Five thousand queens got what they were after. And the TV audience cried their eyes out, morbidly delighted to find there were people even worse off than they were, and so *they* got what they were after.

"*Queen for a Day* was a typical American success story. And if you don't like it, either try to change the rules of the game, or go back where you came from."

Let's Make a Deal

NBC: 1963–1968
ABC: 1968–1976
SYNDICATED: 1971–1976, 1984–

"I'm in inner turmoil," confessed Monty Hall, the longtime host of TV's *Let's Make a Deal*, to *TV Guide* in 1984.

"I have suffered. I know what I am as a performer, and yet no one takes me seriously. I know what I am capable of, and yet I am stereotyped. I became so closely identified with *Let's Make a Deal* that people started putting me in the same category as the contestants.

"If they had referred to me as the man who handles the idiots jumping up and down, that would have been okay.... I'm tired of being identified as just another mindless game show host."

Monty Hall's claims of inner torture must, of course, be taken with a grain of salt, considering that he happily served as host for all the versions of *Let's Make a Deal* during its on-again, off-again run through the sixties, seventies, and eighties. And, of course, if the show's contestants knew that he thought of them as "idiots jumping up and down," they

might have a different deal in mind for Monty—one involving a couple of cement shoes and a deep river.

Deal had a simple premise and a great gimmick: All the contestants were chosen from that day's studio audience. In order to sit down on the "trading floor," one merely had to don a costume; the more outlandish, the better. Your average Halloween-style outfit wouldn't cut it on *Let's Make a Deal*. Aspiring contestants were well advised to try costumes that made them look like idiots—and not to forget that all-important jumping up and down.

One also had to bring along an item of questionable value to "trade" with Monty, who would then lead the contestant through a pricing game or two, giving him or her the opportunity to trade for "what's inside the box" or "what's behind the curtain."

Cars, trips, and major appliances were the things that set contestants jumping up and down in paroxysms of joy—a practice that the staff of *Let's Make a Deal* encour-

Monty Hall grins on *Let's Make a Deal*. Diane Arbus herself would have been proud of this oddly disturbing shot, with the wizened hands applauding in the foreground, and the eerily serene mannequin in the back, looking placidly skyward. *Hatos-Hall Productions*

aged. But hidden behind each colorful curtain or carton might be a "zonk"—a prize of no intrinsic value whatsoever. Zonks usually were meant to be humorous, but contestants who traded a Broyhill living room set for a 12-foot rocking chair, a broken-down tractor, or a live goat weren't too amused.

Let's Make a Deal was also the vehicle that created the first big "game show model"—a pretty woman who makes her living leaning on refrigerators, "outlining" boxes of cake mix with shapely fingertips, and waving at new Toyotas. Carol Merrill, *Deal*'s model, gained a cult following who knew her as "the lovely Carol Merrill" and never grew tired of seeing their heroine pointing at prizes of every description. Merrill even made a comeback on *Late Night with David Letterman*, sitting for an interview and outlining a few kitchen appliances for old times' sake.

(Merrill's star was eclipsed, of course, in the 1980s, when *Wheel of Fortune* model Vanna White achieved such popularity that major publications clamored for interviews and she ended up gracing the covers of both *Newsweek* and *Playboy*.)

The show was a hit ever since its introduction on NBC in 1963, and when it moved to ABC in 1968, its power was so potent that NBC's whole daytime schedule suffered.

At times, viewers might have mistaken Monty Hall for one of the idiots jumping up and down. On one telecast, which the venerable host remembers as being "my most embarrassing moment," Hall was making some big deals with contestants in the usual ridiculous costumes. He offered a man in a sailor suit $200 if he could produce a bosun's whistle, and a Chinese-clad woman $200 if she had any Chinese money. Spying a woman carrying a baby bottle, he took it from her and said, "Show me another nipple, and I'll give you $200!"

The laughter ran through the credits and didn't stop until the show went off the air that day.

When ABC dropped the nightowl *Deal* in 1971, it continued and did very well in syndication until both versions went off the air in 1976. The country couldn't live too long without seeing people dressed as bananas and hula girls, however, and Hall hosted a Canadian revival of the show in the early 1980s. That lasted just long enough to perk up NBC's interest all over again—some twenty years after the show had debuted on the network—and in late 1983 Hall and the Peacock tried to Make a Deal among themselves.

"I told NBC I had already done 4,000 episodes of *Let's Make a Deal* and if they wanted me they had to give me something else, like guest shots and variety show skits. Maybe the Rose Bowl. I don't mind crumbs, but I want a *lot* of crumbs," said Hall hopefully.

NBC, apparently, zonked him.

Above It's time for greed and hilarity when Monty Hall twists the dials on this Mr. Robot, sending the mechanial man home with a prize or a zonk on *Let's Make a Deal.* *Below* A crayon, a gorilla, and a banana slug it out with "TV's big dealer . . . Monty Hall!" *Hatos-Hall Productions*

The thrill of victory, the agony of defeat. Three high rollers find that their gamble paid off on *Let's Make a Deal,* while the two "unflappable flappers" don't look nearly as excited with their prize. Could they have traded a world cruise for a lifetime supply of Rice-A-Roni? *Hatos-Hall Productions*

That fall, Hall was back in syndication (sans Carol Merrill) with *The All-New Let's Make a Deal*. The chief difference between the *All-New* and the good old versions was the invention of a few new appliances to give away—food processors, microwaves, and such—but the basic structure stayed the same: excitable contestants, suburban-costume-party attire, boldfaced greed, and Monty Hall.

The "inner turmoil" of Monty Hall couldn't have been so bad after all. Although he might have professed nothing but contempt for the line of work that made him famous, Monty Hall's twenty-year tenure was reminiscent of another long-running game show—*The Price Is Right*.

The Gong Show

NBC (daytime version): 1976–78
SYNDICATED (nighttime version): 1976–80

Amateur hours, those TV staples of the Fabulous Fifties, seemed as dead as the TV western in the 1970s. Yet in 1976, the hottest and most-discussed new show on TV was another amateur hour, updated for a nastier America. You weren't likely to see a barbershop quartet on *The Gong Show*. *Butchershop* was more like it.

One thing was for sure. In an industry where new shows are usually pale carbons of other successful programs, *The Gong Show* was a red-blooded original:

• A hideously obese woman in a revealing outfit grins at a panel of tuxedoed judges as music begins. She begins burping in time to the music. The audience howls.

• Two teenage girls with soulful eyes sit on the studio floor Indian-style while fellating large Popsicles. The audience howls.

• An elderly man with a body like a dessicated, dehydrated turkey minces and pirouettes around the stage in a classical ballet, a frilly tutu barely masking his geriatric genitalia. The audience howls.

• Count Banjola, a man dressed as a vampire, hangs suspended by his feet while plucking a tune on a banjo. The audience howls.

• Another hideously obese woman (fat women were always a hit on *The Gong Show* during its heyday) does a suggestive go-go dance while clad in a string bikini. The audience howls.

And then there were the acts that were deemed too much for even *The Gong Show*. The chicken that had a bowel movement in extreme close-up. The man who extinguished candles with fart power. The man dressed as Christ, who hung on a cross while he sang "Release Me."

TV fans will recognize the visionary philosophy of Chuck Barris behind these divertissements— Barris, the man whose previous TV wallows included *The Dating Game*, *The Newlywed Game*, and a glittering piece of short-lived trash called *How's Your Mother-in-Law?*

People dubbed him "The Sultan of Sadism." *Us* referred to the show as "Your Show of Schmoes" and "a sadomasochist's version of Disneyland." In the words of Liberace, though, Barris cried all the way to the bank; his brain-damaged brainchild stood with *Laverne & Shirley* and *Three's Company* as one of the most profitable hits of the late seventies.

By the time *TV Guide* came nosing around for a profile on this modern P.T. Barnacle, Barris was self-effacing and a bit matter-of-fact about his accomplishment. "It's a simple, vaudevillelike variety show," he said. "People always like to see other people fed to the lions. To get out there and get tormented, that takes guts. It's reassuring to find there is somebody unhappier than you are."

Barris and his partner, Chris Bearde, might have been famous to TV audiences for puerile pandering, but to television executives, they were the men with the keys to the mint, producing inexpensive programs that created millions in revenue. With price tags uppermost in their minds, Bearde and Barris hit upon the notion that a modern-day variety hour would be incredibly cheap to produce, so they began auditioning rank amateurs who could sing "Feelings," imitate Edward G. Robinson, or do a passable version of the Latin Hustle. The results were disappointing. "There just wasn't enough good talent to sustain even

one year," moaned Barris, finding the rank amateurs a little too rank to stomach.

Bearde, like a chip off the old Barris blockhead, had the million-dollar idea first. "Wouldn't it be great with craze-o's? Fill your show with crazed talent. Then put in a panel of celebrities and when things get too heavy, the panel gongs them. Like the hook in vaudeville. I'd call it *The Gong Show*."

And thus was the show born, and Chuckie Baby became known in the entertainment industry as King Gong. Barris, ever concerned with the philosophical metaphor, defended his baby: "Is somebody singing with a lampshade on her head worse than a pistol-whipping on a detective show? I never considered taste or intelligence in my shows. My thrust was always entertaining the lowest common denominator."

ABC, the network that had clawed its way from the cellar to the top in the seventies with shows like *Charlie's Angels* and *Three's Company*, also had an interest in the lowest common denominator of American society. It was natural that ABC was the only network to express an interest in *Gong*, and the web bought the pilot, which featured Gary Owens as host and *Laugh-In* alumni like Arte Johnson, Jo Anne Worley, and Richard Dawson as the black-tie, gong-wielding panelists. The set consisted mostly of a desk for the celebrities, a small stage, and a giant Chinese-style gong displayed prominently. It was rung often, much to the audience's delight.

Barris knew that he had tapped into *something*, and saw *The Gong Show* as his ticket back into the big bucks of daytime TV. It was NBC that bought a daytime version, and Barris immediately seized control of the NBC show, leaving Bearde to supervise the nighttime version.

One of the first things that happened on the daytime show was the bouncing of host Gary Owens. It would have been inconceivable to put the mondo-bizarro *Gong Show* in the hands of a stalwart host like Wink Martindale or Bill Cullen; the network tried several hosts (including John Barbour of *Real People*, who was no stranger to schlock himself) before coming back to producer/novelist/entrepreneur Barris himself. Soon the off-camera Svengali was a personality in his own right: the tweed-hatted Chuckie Baby.

And the audience loved him. Even the critics agreed that Barris was probably the only host who could present a check for $516.32 to the winning contestant while a midget raced around the stage, scattering confetti on winners and losers alike. Gary Owens' impossibly deep voice couldn't compete with Chuckie Baby's twitches, hand-clapping, and nervous laughter. After a year Owens was off the nighttime version, as was cocreator Chris Bearde. They had both been replaced by Barris.

The Gong Show was a smash in both the daytime and nighttime versions. (The evening show was a virtual duplicate of the daytime version, only the prize was raised to a magnanimous $712.05.) Certainly there was no shortage of contestants; the freakish and the pathetic began streaming out of the woodwork.

Barris's production company began seeing hundreds of aspiring *Gong Show* contestants every week, selecting the 65 lucky people who would get their Warholish fifteen minutes of fame on that week's ten shows. In a sense, the mod geek-show realm of Andy Warhol's Factory had expanded. During the Bicentennial year, Chuckie Baby was hotter than the Statue of Liberty.

Several panelists established themselves early as supernovas of the *Gong Show* universe. The raucous, coarse attempts at humor made by comedienne Jaye P. Morgan fit in perfectly with the proceedings, as did the contributions of Phyllis Diller and Rip Taylor. (Even the most simpleminded viewer must have noted the irony in the likes of *Rip Taylor* passing judgment on another human being's talent.)

A few other regulars formed the Supreme Court of *Gong* judges. Longtime L.A. Dodger Steve Garvey sat stiffly in his tuxedo, clutching his gong mallet and grinning uncertainly at everything that unfolded around him. Most embarrassing of all was the sight of Dr. Joyce Brothers, that expert on human nature and exporter of empathy, joyfully gonging contestant after contestant.

Most unbelievably, a few stars actually *did* emerge from the *Gong Show* universe. Barris delighted in using his staff and stagehands as talent (despite angry memos from the network to cease and desist with the stagehands), and one of them, who became known as Gene-Gene the Dancing Machine, regularly interrupted the show with his spastic break-dancing antics. Murray Langston forged a minor career as the Unknown Comic, a joker with gold chains, a white disco suit, and a brown paper bag over his head. Only one contestant went on to any kind of a significant career: After Cheryl Lynn appeared on *Gong* singing "You Are So Beautiful," she was offered several recording contracts and added a brief footnote to the short-lived history of disco music with two hits, "Got to Be Real" and "Star Love."

The show seemed to have run its course after two years on NBC's daytime schedule, although it continued on in its nighttime slot, where viewers still seemed to enjoy Barris's brand of T & A—torture and abuse.

"You can really put yourself out of commission if you cross a certain line," said Barris in 1978. "You can be so distasteful that people will not watch. There's always a lunatic fringe that always will watch, but you don't want just them. When you push people across that line, you lose them."

He pushed them across that line with *The Gong Show Movie*, a 1980 attempt to bring the show to the silver screen. If the film had only focused on the show's acts—including censored footage of Jaye P. Morgan flashing her breasts on camera—it might have done well in neighborhood theaters. Instead, *The Gong Show Movie* was mostly a gong-o-biography, with emphasis on Chuck Barris's tortured private life—a cathartic wallow reminiscent of *All That Jazz*. Unfortunately, Gongmania had already gone the way of mood rings and Peter Frampton albums, leaving hundreds of empty seats in cinemas across America.

It wasn't for lack of a publicity push; *The Gong Show Movie* made its world premiere at the venerable Grauman's Chinese Theater. In true Barris style, the event was a denigration of every glamorous film premiere that preceded it. Limousines were replaced by ambulances, pimpmobiles, and hearses, and guests alighted from their chariots clad in anything but black tie. Army Archerd and Rip Taylor announced the arrivals with an appropriate lack of taste and wit. (As *Hollywood Squares* host Peter Marshall arrived, Taylor noted, "His name sounds like the security guard at a gay bar.")

Other guests included Monsieur La Poof, who doused a candle with *le flatulence* in the film; The Embryo

Twins, two men who sang "Havin' My Baby" while encased in a plastic amniotic sac; three drag queens dressed as nuns; and a virtual embarrassment of fat ladies, who must have been particularly pleased with the eats at the après-screening party.

Caterers worked feverishly to slake the thirsts and hungers of guests with nitrite-rich hot dogs, potato chips, innumerable Hostess snack cakes, and all the all-American junk foods that made for the perfect dinner while watching *The Gong Show*. Barris, meanwhile, entertained onstage with country-western tunes on the guitar. Film critics, of course, joined their TV counterparts in condemning the *Gong* mentality.

The Gong Show continued on in syndication, but new episodes were never made—Chuck Barris seemed to realize that he'd milked the pop culture teat as far as he could.

Until 1986.

In May of that year, small ads began appearing in the good, gray *Wall Street Journal*. Placed by Barris, they were desperately seeking "all stockbrokers, investment bankers, Wall Street attorneys, secretaries, clerks, or anyone working for a Wall Street-related firm to contact us if you're interested in performing in our upcoming show entitled *The Gong Show Goes to Wall Street*."

The stock exchange managed to survive the Crash of '29, but whether it manages to escape the Gong of '86 unscathed is anybody's guess.

The $1.98 Beauty Show

SYNDICATED: 1978–1980

On *The Gong Show*, Chuck Barris earned millions of dollars by making fun of contestants' lack of talent. On *The $1.98 Beauty Show*, he took that successful formula one step farther—he made fun of the contestants themselves.

Got a face that only a mother pit bull could love? Got a body the size of the Lower West Side? Any woman with basketball-sized buttocks was given the chance to parade her assets in hopes of winning the grand prize of $1.98, topped off with a tacky tiara and a "bouquet" of rotting vegetables.

This Who's Who for the Big Beautiful Woman was a parody/travesty of the great American beauty pageant. Every week, a variety of women would strut their stuff in evening gown, talent, and—to the audience's howling delight—swimsuit competition. Although a few token bosomy blondes were included to ensure that *everyone* didn't look like Shelley Winters on a bad day, the big attractions of the *Beauty Show* were cellulite-ridden females who were willing to embarrass themselves on national TV for what was surely the smallest prize ever on any TV game. It made *The Gong Show*'s top prize of $516.32 look like an exercise in largesse.

An exercise in such good taste required just *le* host *juste*, and anyone expecting Alistair Cooke, Dick Cavett, or even Bert Parks was obviously unfamiliar with Chuck Barris's unique artistic sensibility. Executive producer Barris secured the talents of Rip Taylor, a comedian and frequent *Gong*-wielder whose braying voice, poor toupee, and ubiquitous bag of confetti had established him as the stand-up's answer to a Borscht Belt Liberace. In any case, Taylor's fey demeanor clearly demonstrated that he wasn't the best possible judge of feminine pulchritude—which made him the perfect arbiter when it came to humiliating a Lane Bryant refugee in a drooping bikini.

The first telecast, in September 1978, featured an all-star panel—

Erik Estrada, Suzy "Call Me Suzy Chapstick" Chaffee, and former *L.A. Times* columnist Joyce Haber. Judges on future telecasts included Jamie Farr, Patty "Don't Sit Under the Apple Tree" Andrews, and *Gong Show* regular Jaye P. Morgan, whose zealous pursuit of tastelessness provided the perfect counterpoint to Rip Taylor's leers.

The theme of the set was mock elegance gone berserk with chandeliers galore, crushed velvet draperies, and baroque filigree everywhere. A black-tie orchestra serenaded the stocky señoritas as they strutted their stuff in loungewear or performed classical ballet in the talent competition, thudding their way around the stage with all the grace of hippopotami in their death throes.

Overseeing the whole mélange was the porcine Taylor, popping his eyes, twitching his walrus moustache, and generally doing his best to make the proceedings even more humiliating than *The Gong Show*. A studio audience provided the requisite howls and wolf whistles, making the weekly half-hour a Miss Perverse Universe.

Critics, of course, raised their by-now predictable howl while reaching for their up-Chuck cups. And although the Pope didn't have any publicly registered opinion, the Roman Catholic Archdiocese of New York got into the act, putting *The $1.98 Beauty Show* on its list of the fifteen worst shows in a list handed out after Mass one Sunday. Chubby-chasers all over America made the show a minor hit, though; it continued for two profitable years in syndication, giving away what amounted to well over $100 in prizes.

The porky pleasures of *The $1.98 Beauty Show* held America's attention for only a little while, though, and it never quite managed to achieve the household-word status of Barris's other scumfests like *The Newlywed Game* or *The Gong Show*. Rip Taylor, however, survived unscathed, even earning a role in Barris's feature-film attempt at Fellinihood, *The Gong Show Movie*.

Largely forgotten today (except by some exceptionally kinky viewers and a few ultramasochistic television critics), *The $1.98 Beauty Show* still retains a tiny corner in television history, living on in celluloid cellulite immortality.